Digital Filmmaking For Kids

FOR

DUMMIES®

A Wiley Brand

D0730962

Digital Filmmaking For Kids

FOR DUMMIES®
A Wiley Brand

by Nick Willoughby

FOR DUMMIES®
A Wiley Brand

Montrose Reg. Library Dist.
320 S. 2nd St.
Montrose, CO 81401

Digital Filmmaking For Kids For Dummies®

Published by: **John Wiley & Sons, Inc.,** 111 River Street, Hoboken, NJ 07030-5774, www.wiley.com

Copyright © 2015 by John Wiley & Sons, Inc., Hoboken, New Jersey

Published simultaneously in Canada

No part of this publication may be reproduced, stored in a retrieval system or transmitted in any form or by any means, electronic, mechanical, photocopying, recording, scanning or otherwise, except as permitted under Sections 107 or 108 of the 1976 United States Copyright Act, without the prior written permission of the Publisher. Requests to the Publisher for permission should be addressed to the Permissions Department, John Wiley & Sons, Inc., 111 River Street, Hoboken, NJ 07030, (201) 748-6011, fax (201) 748-6008, or online at http://www.wiley.com/go/permissions.

Trademarks: Wiley, For Dummies, the Dummies Man logo, Dummies.com, Making Everything Easier, and related trade dress are trademarks or registered trademarks of John Wiley & Sons, Inc. and may not be used without written permission. All other trademarks are the property of their respective owners. John Wiley & Sons, Inc. is not associated with any product or vendor mentioned in this book.

LIMIT OF LIABILITY/DISCLAIMER OF WARRANTY: THE PUBLISHER AND THE AUTHOR MAKE NO REPRESENTATIONS OR WARRANTIES WITH RESPECT TO THE ACCURACY OR COMPLETENESS OF THE CONTENTS OF THIS WORK AND SPECIFICALLY DISCLAIM ALL WARRANTIES, INCLUDING WITHOUT LIMITATION WARRANTIES OF FITNESS FOR A PARTICULAR PURPOSE. NO WARRANTY MAY BE CREATED OR EXTENDED BY SALES OR PROMOTIONAL MATERIALS. THE ADVICE AND STRATEGIES CONTAINED HEREIN MAY NOT BE SUITABLE FOR EVERY SITUATION. THIS WORK IS SOLD WITH THE UNDERSTANDING THAT THE PUBLISHER IS NOT ENGAGED IN RENDERING LEGAL, ACCOUNTING, OR OTHER PROFESSIONAL SERVICES. IF PROFESSIONAL ASSISTANCE IS REQUIRED, THE SERVICES OF A COMPETENT PROFESSIONAL PERSON SHOULD BE SOUGHT. NEITHER THE PUBLISHER NOR THE AUTHOR SHALL BE LIABLE FOR DAMAGES ARISING HEREFROM. THE FACT THAT AN ORGANIZATION OR WEBSITE IS REFERRED TO IN THIS WORK AS A CITATION AND/OR A POTENTIAL SOURCE OF FURTHER INFORMATION DOES NOT MEAN THAT THE AUTHOR OR THE PUBLISHER ENDORSES THE INFORMATION THE ORGANIZATION OR WEBSITE MAY PROVIDE OR RECOMMENDATIONS IT MAY MAKE. FURTHER, READERS SHOULD BE AWARE THAT INTERNET WEBSITES LISTED IN THIS WORK MAY HAVE CHANGED OR DISAPPEARED BETWEEN WHEN THIS WORK WAS WRITTEN AND WHEN IT IS READ.

For general information on our other products and services, please contact our Customer Care Department within the U.S. at 877-762-2974, outside the U.S. at 317-572-3993, or fax 317-572-4002. For technical support, please visit www.wiley.com/techsupport.

Wiley publishes in a variety of print and electronic formats and by print-on-demand. Some material included with standard print versions of this book may not be included in e-books or in print-on-demand. If this book refers to media such as a CD or DVD that is not included in the version you purchased, you may download this material at http://booksupport.wiley.com. For more information about Wiley products, visit www.wiley.com.

Library of Congress Control Number: 2015937646

ISBN 978-1-119-02740-9 (pbk); ISBN 978-1-119-02747-8 (ebk); ISBN 978-1-119-02745-4 (ebk)

Manufactured in the United States of America

10 9 8 7 6 5 4 3 2 1

Contents at a Glance

Table of Contents

Introduction

So you want to be a filmmaker? Have you ever watched a film or a TV show and wondered how they made it and what it would be like to make your own? Well, you picked up the right book — this is where your filmmaking journey starts.

Digital filmmaking is the process of creating and telling a story or presenting information through the art of film using digital video cameras. Basically, it's a way creative people like you can turn the ideas in your heads into films audiences can watch on movie screens, TVs, or computers. The filmmaking process can take weeks, months, and even years, depending on the length and complexity of the film being made. It involves taking an idea, turning it into a story and a script, storyboarding the script into a series of images, recording the actors performing the script using video cameras and microphones, transferring the video clips from the camera to a computer, and editing the footage into the final film for the audience to enjoy. It may sound like a complicated process, but it's not, really — it's fun, and I'm sure you'll enjoy every moment.

There are thousands of filmmakers in the world, living their dreams of making films and documentaries every day. You could be one of them! *Digital Filmmaking For Kids For Dummies* introduces you to the magical world of filmmaking and guides you through the process of making your own films to share with your family and friends.

About This Book

There aren't many places where you can discover and develop filmmaking knowledge and skills and then practically apply them to your own film projects. In *Digital Filmmaking For Kids For Dummies,* I give you all the knowledge and skills you need and guide you through the filmmaking process step by step.

They say a wise person learns from his mistakes and a clever person learns from other people's mistakes. I've learned everything I know from working in different roles within the filmmaking industry, and the mistakes I made along the way helped me develop my skills and made me better at what I do. The great thing about this book is that I share with you the tips and techniques that I learned, which saves you having to make the same mistakes I did.

In this book, you

- ✔ Explore the different types of camera shots and angles you can use in your films.

- ✔ Discover how to record sound using onboard and external microphones.

- ✔ Find out about how to light your scenes and add mood using natural light and extra lights.

- ✔ Edit your own films together using the editing tool on your computer.

- ✔ Create, film, and edit your own 60-second film trailer.

- ✔ Explore ways to share your films with others, including uploading your films to YouTube.

- ✔ Create, film, and edit your own info film or documentary.

- ✔ Audition people to play the characters in your film.

- ✔ Create a story, write a script, create a storyboard, and then film and edit your own short film.

It's better to understand the process and techniques of filmmaking before you go out and make your first film. This book helps you gain this understanding, as well as the following:

- ✔ **Inspiration:** I help you think of ideas and stories to tell through film and find ways of making your camera shots look great.

- ✔ **Knowledge:** I give you the information you need to get the best from your ideas and stories and turn them into amazing films.

- ✔ **Skills:** I show you ways to enhance and improve the look and sound of your films through camera and microphone techniques.

- ✔ **Results:** I explain how to edit everything you've filmed together and bring it to life in the editing tool to make a film you are proud to share with your family and friends.

Foolish Assumptions

You may know a little bit about me (especially if you've read the "About the Author" section at the back of this book), but I know nothing about you. Still, to write this book I had to make a few guesses and assumptions about the things you already know about filmmaking and about the experience you may have had before reading this book. These foolish assumptions helped me to decide what to include in this book.

I assume that you're interested in making films, which is not a difficult assumption since otherwise you wouldn't have picked this book up in the first place. Maybe you've been involved in filmmaking before reading this book, or maybe you never used a video camera before. Either way, this book can help you.

Also, I assume you have access to a digital video camera, whether it be a camcorder you own, a video camera on your cellphone, or someone else's camera you can borrow. Even if you don't have access to a digital video camera right now, don't worry — you'll still find this book useful.

Finally, I assume you're new to filmmaking and that you want to learn the whole process of making a film from start to finish. Of course, even if you're a professional or have made films before, I'm sure you'll find this book useful, even if only to refresh your knowledge and skills.

Icons Used in This Book

As you read through the projects in this book, you will notice a few icons as shown below:

The Remember icon gives you a little reminder about important things to remember when you make your films.

This icon will appear when I am explaining technical information and techniques.

![TIP]

I use the Tip icon when I have information or advice that could help you with your film project.

![WARNING!]

If there is something that could be dangerous or should be avoided, the Warning icon will appear.

Beyond the Book

I have made available a lot of extra content that you won't find in this book. Go online to find the following:

✔ **Online articles covering additional topics at**

www.dummies.com/extras/digitalfilmmakingforkids

Here you'll find videos where I demonstrate some of the ideas discussed in this book and give you some tips to help you make your films.

✔ **An online Cheat Sheet for digital filmmaking is available at**

www.dummies.com/cheatsheet/digitalfilmmakingforkidsfd

Here you can find a list of notes that you can quickly read to help you make your film.

✔ **Example footage and clips are available at**

www.dummies.com/go/digitalfilmmakingforkidsfd

Becoming a filmmaker is a very visual experience, which means that sometimes you need to see examples of what I am explaining. For that reason, I have included example footage and clips filmed by our crew when making their films.

✔ **Updates to this book, if there are any, can be found at**

www.dummies.com/extras/digitalfilmmakingforkids.

Where to Go from Here

Digital Filmmaking For Kids For Dummies will help launch you into the filmmaking world and give you the confidence you need to get out there and turn your ideas into films. After you have read this book, you may wish to study this topic further at college or look into any film courses near you. Whatever you decide to do next, I encourage you to keep watching films to get inspiration and techniques from, and to keep making your own films as that is the best way to develop as a filmmaker.

It's now time to start your filmmaking journey. I'm really excited to be able to introduce you to the filmmaking world and to guide you through making your own films.

This book is made up of projects, which are designed for you to be able to jump to different stages of the filmmaking process. If you already understand how your camera works, the different types of camera shots, the best way to record sound, and how to edit a film, then you can jump to Part II, Part III, or Part IV, as you like. You can always come back to Part I later.

Even if you're an experienced filmmaker, however, I recommend starting at Project 0 and working your way through all the projects in order. If you jump ahead, you may miss something really important. In Part I, for example, I share some great ways to enhance the look and sound of your film, which you will find this information very useful in Parts II, III, and IV.

Week 1
The Basic Digital Filmmaking Process

This week you'll . . .

For Dummies can help you get started with lots of subjects. Visit www.dummies.com to learn more.

Getting Started with Digital Filmmaking

Welcome to *Digital Filmmaking for Kids For Dummies.* What is digital filmmaking and how is it different from ordinary film-making? Good question! Many years ago, perhaps before you were born, films were captured using cameras that recorded a series of still images to a reel of film or tape that ran through the camera. These reels were then cut together by hand, which was a very long and complicated process. Back then, fewer people were able to make high-quality films due to the cost of the equipment and production.

Digital filmmaking is simpler and less expensive than traditional filmmaking because digital cameras are able to capture images digitally through electronic chips, which send the images to media cards or hard drives and not to reels of film, which are expensive to buy and can't be reused. The importing and editing process is also simpler because each section or clip of recorded video is imported and edited as separate files, making the editing process quicker and more efficient.

Some filmmakers still prefer traditional filmmaking to digital filmmaking because they prefer the look of the images captured with old, traditional film cameras. That look used to be hard to replicate with digital cameras, but things are changing. Some of the latest digital cinema cameras produce unbelievably beautiful footage.

The introduction of digital cameras has opened up opportunities for future filmmakers like you to get your films made and get them seen. It's never been easier or cheaper to turn ideas and stories into films. Just look at the number of short films on YouTube and Vimeo — we live in a creative world!

With the skills and tips you learn in this book, you will be turning your ideas and stories into films to share with your family and friends.

The Filmmaking Process

The filmmaking process can be divided up into five main stages:

- ✔ Development
- ✔ Pre-production
- ✔ Production
- ✔ Post-production
- ✔ Distribution

If you imagine the filmmaking process as a journey, these five main stages are stops on the way. You can't get to your final destination unless you stop at each of these places along the way. Each of these stages are discussed in the next few sections.

Development

This is one of the most important areas of the filmmaking process, and it can be one of the hardest. too. It's usually the longest part of filmmaking, because it's important to get the concept and the story right before moving into the production phase. Development can be rushed, however, and is sometimes skipped altogether, although this leaves the story undeveloped, which can cause problems for the filmmaker later in the pre-production stage. The development stage involves creating ideas and building the story so that it's ready to take into pre-production.

In the development stage, the filmmaker comes up with themes and ideas in order to create a story with a good beginning, middle, and end. This story is then used to create a script for the actors to work from and a storyboard for the director and crew to work from.

Pre-production

This stage uses the idea, story, script, and storyboard created in the development stage to prepare for the production stage. In pre-production, everything is planned for as much as possible. If this stage is rushed or skipped, something may go wrong during the production stage, and it could take longer to film.

In the pre-production stage, actors are cast for the characters in the film, locations are found and sets are built for each scene, each filming day is planned and scheduled, and rehearsals for the actors are organized. The time and attention spent at this stage saves time in the production and post-production stages.

Production

The production stage is where the story and characters come to life through film. This stage relies heavily on the previous stages: If the story and script aren't finalized or if no actors have been cast or no locations chosen, filming can't begin.

The production stage starts with running rehearsals for the actors to learn their lines and to develop their characters. During production, camera equipment is set up on location, and the planned scenes are filmed. The final stage of production is to review the filmed footage to make sure all scenes and necessary shots have been captured, and that the footage looks good enough to pass on to the post-production stage.

Post-production

The post-production stage is where the footage captured during production is pieced together to tell the story through editing. This stage is exciting: The filmmaker gets to see the results of all the hard work put into the previous stages and to watch the film come together in the editing tool.

The post-production stage starts with importing and editing the footage captured during filming in an editing program, such as iMovie, on a computer. When all footage is imported and edited together, music and sound effects can be added and the footage can be enhanced with color and effects ready to be distributed.

Traditional forms of film editing are *linear,* meaning that they involve searching through reels of tape to edit film in sequence. Video-editing programs, such as iMovie, Windows Movie Maker, Final Cut, and Adobe Premiere, are known as *non-linear editors (NLE)* because they are freer; with them, you can view and edit video footage in a timeline in any order you like.

Distribution

Distribution is the final stage in the filmmaking journey. At this point, the film has been produced and edited, and it's ready for the audience to enjoy. This can be a worrying time for the film-maker because the film will be viewed by an audience who will supply comments and reviews. This is the first point at which the filmmaker will get to see an audience's response to the film.

Most mainstream films are first distributed to cinemas and then released on DVD, online streaming services, and television later. Low-budget films, on the other hand, don't always get a cinema release. Instead, they first appear at film festivals and are then released to online video-hosting sites (and sometimes DVD) later.

Lights, Camera, What?

As you read through this book there will be some words that are new to you. Here I've created a list of filmmaking-related terms and their meanings. If you're ever unclear about a word I've used in this book, you can refer to this list.

Action: A term called by the director during the filming of a scene to let cast and crew that a take has started.

Angle: The position of the camera with respect to the subject.

Blockbuster: A large-scale film with a high production budget usually released globally into cinemas.

Boom: A long pole with a microphone attached. Booms are usually held above the actors to record sound in a scene.

Camcorder: A video camera, which is a device used to record video footage.

Camera phone: A cellphone device that can capture still images and record video footage.

Cast: The group of actors appearing in a film or video.

Character: A person within a story, usually fictional.

Clapperboard: A board on which details of the film shoot are written, which is held in front of the camera to introduce a scene during filming. Traditionally chalk was used to write the details on the clapperboard but now marker pens are used. A clapperboard is sometimes referred to as a *slate*.

Costume: Clothes worn by the actors during filming.

Crew: A group of people behind the scenes or behind the camera who are involved in the making of a film or video.

Cut: A term is called by the director during filming to let the cast and crew know that a take is over.

Development: The process of building and creating the film.

Dialogue: The words spoken among the characters in a film or video.

Director: The person who works with actors and crew when filming to help tell the story through their performance and the shots captured.

Editing: The process of putting the film footage and clips together after filming.

Editing tool: The software on a computer used to edit video.

Effect: A visual or audio technique used to enhance or change the look or sound of a video clip. Effects can be added during filming or when editing.

Establishing shot: This is the first shot to appear in a new scene, which "establishes" for the viewer the setting of the scene.

Filmmaker: The person who creates a film or movie.

Fictional film: A film based on a story that is imagined by the writer and not normally based on fact.

FireWire cable: A way of transferring data and video footage from a camera to a computer. FireWire connections can also be referred to as IEEE 1394.

Focus: The sharpness of an image.

Frame: A still image taken from the many images captured within a video clip or film footage.

Lens: A device attached to the camera that uses glass to focus on a subject.

Lighting: Devices that provide light to a scene.

Lines: Character dialogue or words in the script performed by the actors.

Location: A place or area used to film a scene.

Media card: A storage device that captures and holds the information or video being recorded by the camera.

Microphone: A device used to record sound when filming.

Monitor: A mini TV screen usually used to view what the camera captures as it films or to review what already has been recorded.

Nonfictional film: A documentary film created using factual information or real events starring real people involved in the events.

Post-production: The work put into a movie after filming.

Prop: Any item used by an actor in a scene or that is otherwise involved in the film.

Reel: A length of filmstrip wrapped around a metal wheel so as to be more easily viewed on a projector. Film was the medium used to record motion pictures before the age of digital video (and is still used in increasingly rare cases), but because only a portion of all cinemas have upgraded to digital projectors, even digitally shot movies are often still distributed on film reels. An average movie requires three to five reels of film.

Scene: A series of shots filmed at one location to tell a section of the main story.

Schedule: A plan of the day's filming that shows the times and details of shots to be filmed.

Script: A document showing the details of a story that is to be filmed, including the scenes and dialogue to be performed by the actors.

Set: An area built and constructed where a scene can be filmed.

Shoot: To film or record video footage.

Shot: One section of footage recorded by the camera from start to finish.

Shot list: A list used by the crew showing the shots to be filmed within a scene.

Sound effects: Sounds added to a film when editing.

Storyboard: A series of images created before filming to plan the shots to filmed.

Subject: The person or object being filmed.

Take: One recorded performance of a scene during filming. A filmmaker could expect to shoot tens or hundreds of takes per scene (depending on the length of a scene).

USB cable: A way of transferring data or video footage from a camera to a computer.

Voiceover: A recorded voice used in a film or documentary. The speaker is not shown.

Zoom: The magnification of an object or subject when filming that makes the subject appear to be closer or farther away.

A Filmmaker's Tools

A filmmaker can spend a fortune on all the different tools available to make films. However, to get started, a filmmaker needs only a few basic tools, most of which are relatively inexpensive:

- **Video camera:** Without a video camera, there is no film. A video camera captures the picture and audio and stores them on a media card, hard drive, or tape, ready to be imported and edited later.

- **Microphone:** The microphone picks up sound waves and converts them into signals that can be understood by the camera, which are then recorded along with the picture onto a media card, hard drive, or tape.

- **Light source:** Your subjects need to be seen by your audience, so a light source is quite important. The light source could be a natural one, like the sun, or an artificial one, like the light from a lamp.

- **Editing tool:** An editing tool is a computer program into which you import video footage, slice it up, and arrange into an order suitable for viewing by your audience.

- **Tripod:** A tripod is a great tool for keeping the camera steady in a fixed position. It can be used to smoothly film moving subjects from left to right or up and down.

- **Media card/tape:** Means of storing video footage captured by the camera.

- **Headphones:** A device that can be plugged into a video camera or external sound recorder to monitor the quality of the audio being recorded.

Life as a Filmmaker

Ever since I was a young boy I've enjoyed being creative. I used to write my own plays and sketches and perform them in front of my family and friends. My sister and I would record our own radio shows. I would even turn the act of making cheese on toast into a TV show. Later, when it came to deciding what I would choose as a career, I was unsure which path to take, and because it seemed sensible to try to fit in, I decided to work with computers. Back then, I thought that being an actor or filmmaker wasn't a real job. In the first five years of my career, however, I changed jobs more than ten times — something was wrong! Those so-called "sensible and normal" jobs didn't make me happy. It occurred to me that I wouldn't be happy until I was using the creative brain I was born with. I then made the decision to follow my dream to be involved in the TV and film industry. Now filmmaking is my life, my job, and my hobby — I love it!

Of course, like every job, filmmaking can be stressful. You can work long hours. There's often too much to do and too little time or money to do it. Even so, the good aspects of working in the film industry outnumber the negative ones. No one day is the same as the next; that's one of the things I love about the filmmaking industry. The majority of the work I get is for corporate clients. This is great, but it's perhaps less exciting than working on dramatic or story-based films. Corporate filmmaking usually includes filming talking heads — often just a mid shot of someone talking to the camera delivering a message or conveying information about a subject. Other work includes promotional videos, charity films, training videos, product videos, filmed events, and short films.

One the other exciting things about being a filmmaker is being able to work on a project from start to finish. I enjoy all aspects of filmmaking — from coming up with ideas and developing stories to filming productions and importing and editing. It's a great feeling to bring a film to completion and to watch the completed work (and to watch other people's reactions to it). The filmmaking industry is all about using your creative skills to provide entertainment and present information to others using the art of film.

My only regret is that I didn't become a filmmaker sooner — I wish I hadn't undergone that five-year period I spent doing the wrong job. Never let anyone tell you that you can't do something. There's a job out there — filmmaker or pilot or doctor — for everyone. Life's too short to follow someone else's dreams.

Over the course of this book, I guide you through the process of making films: making your own trailer, documentary, and short narrative film. Along the way, I pass on all the filmmaking knowledge that I've learned over the many years I have been involved in the industry.

Getting to Know Your Camera

Imagine living in the 1920s when home video cameras had only recently been invented and were big, basic, and very expensive. This meant that only very few people could make their own movies.

Things have changed a lot since then with the introduction of digital camcorders and even more recently the camera phone. Now more people are able to record video anywhere they go, either on a camcorder or a camera on a phone. Even digital still cameras record great quality video, which just increases the options you have to make your own films.

Just take a moment to think of all the really clever people who were involved in making the video camera what it is today so that we can create our own films at home — thank you, clever people!

You don't have to have a $50,000 camera to make your own film; you can make it with any video camera you have access to. You don't even have to own a camera as long as you have access to someone else's. I started writing films before I had a camera, and I invited my friends to help me make them with their cameras. A good filmmaker uses the skills of people around them to make his or her films.

Using someone else's camera equipment is a fine way to begin filming inexpensively. However, always be sure you have permission to use camera equipment if it belongs to someone else.

As a filmmaker, you can choose to either shoot a film yourself or you can invite other people to operate the camera while you direct. Either option is fine. Your choice may depend on what you're filming and whether you need help. Many documentaries, for instance, are both shot and directed by the filmmaker in order to simplify and reduce the number of people around when filming. Usually, more people are needed to shoot a film in which dialogue needs to be recorded and lighting set up. Also, don't disregard the value of additional opinions: Having people working with you can make the filming process easier, quicker, and more enjoyable.

How Does Your Camera Work?

Don't worry: I'm not going to go into great detail here but it's useful to know the basics of how your camera works.

A video camera works in a way that's similar way to the way your eye works. Your eye sees things as a series of still images or *frames* and your brain then puts them together so quickly it looks like smooth movement — it's clever stuff, isn't it? The camera does a very similar thing: It captures movement in a series of frames. In cameras, this movement is measured in *frames per second.* (See Figure 1-1.)

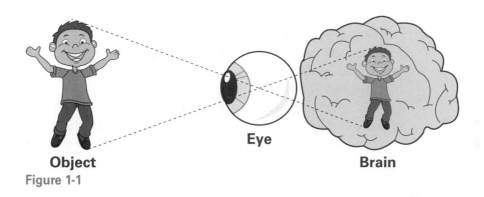

Object   **Eye**   **Brain**

Figure 1-1

Also, like your eye, the camera records the images using light from the scene you are filming. The light enters through the lens and the images are captured by a microchip inside the digital video camera. These images are then sent to your media card or tape. Figure 1-2 shows how a digital video camera records an image to a media card or disk.

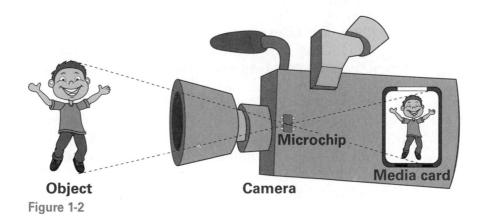

Object   **Camera**

Figure 1-2

The introduction of digital video cameras has made the filmmaking process simpler and less expensive. Traditional film cameras captured film footage as a series of still images onto a light-sensitive reel of tape running through the camera. This reel of tape would be expensive to buy and couldn't be reused. It also made setting up and checking shots difficult because there was no easy way of playing back the footage you had captured without going through the complex process of editing those reels of tape. Traditional film cameras create what I call a "cinematic" look, however, allowing for a softer look to the image than you can get with digital video. With traditional cameras, you can blur backgrounds, for example, making your subject stand out. It's more difficult to get this cinematic look with a digital video camera, especially with lower-range camcorders, which often have trouble dealing with the lighter and darker areas of a shot, and whose image tends to be sharper and more crisp.

Deciding on a Camera to Use

Digital video cameras vary in price, size, and quality. For under $100, you can buy a compact HD camcorder that will record great video, but it may not have all the functions a professional filmmaker would expect. At the other extreme, you can find video cameras that cost over $50,000, which are used to shoot blockbuster movies — but even these have their disadvantages.

As a filmmaker, I like to use different types of digital video cameras for different reasons. In the following list, I describe the different types of digital video cameras currently available:

✔ **Camera phones:** A camera phone is a cellphone that is able to capture still images and video footage. (See Figure 1-3.) Camera phones are more lightweight and compact, which makes it easier to capture video in smaller spaces. The latest camera phones can capture stunning photos and video footage and have helped to reduce the need for digital compact cameras.

Camera phones don't offer the best quality for picture or sound, but they're great for capturing video simply and quickly.

Because camera phones are perfect for capturing offhand moments you couldn't film with larger, more professional cameras, I use them occasionally to capture video and images for behind-the-scenes projects.

Figure 1-3

✔ **Camcorders:** A camcorder (see Figure 1-4) is a portable hand-held video camera designed to record video and audio. Camcorders usually have lenses built into the camera body and are designed to make recording video quicker and more simple. Over the years, camcorders have become more affordable and now offer better video and sound quality than ever before.

There are many types of camcorders to choose from, starting with basic compact cameras around $100 shooting all the way up to the broadcast cameras above $50,000. The general breakdown is into two broad categories, as follows:

● *Affordable camcorders:* Recently, camcorders have become more affordable, which is great news for home-video

Figure 1-4

filmmakers. The affordable range of camcorders offers some great features and fantastic quality. Most of the cameras in this range offer "automatic" functions such as autofocus, which searches for the subject in the scene you're filming and focuses on that subject, rather than on things in the background. Some of these camcorders have face-detection features so that the camera focuses on the people in the shot. Other nice features include *auto-iris,* which adjusts the brightness of the picture depending on the amount of light available, and *auto–white-balance,* which adjusts how warm or cold the picture looks, depending on what is needed in the scene.

Camcorders in this range are small, light, easy to work with, and are great for shooting scenes quickly, which is why they are perfect for shooting home videos.

- *Professional camcorders:* Professional filmmakers need more from their cameras than most home video makers do. The ability to manually control all the settings on a camcorder is very useful to a professional filmmaker because they like to be able to choose what to focus on and how bright or warm the picture should look. The camcorders in this range are normally used by news teams to record outside broadcasts, and by production companies for corporate film projects.

Usually, the higher you go up in the range of professional camcorders, the bigger the cameras get and the more manual features they have. The bigger camcorders are heavier and can take longer to set up. The quality of the lens on the camcorder normally increases along with the quality of the picture and sound, too.

Digital video cameras record and store the footage captured through the lens onto a media device. Recently manufactured cameras record onto media cards — cards that hold digital information that can be read by your computer when editing — whereas older digital cameras record onto other media, often tape cassettes, which record data onto a reel of tape that can be played back through the camera and imported onto a computer using a cable from the camera.

I use camcorders for most of my corporate film projects, event filming, and interviews for a number of reasons: They can be easier and quicker to set up; they offer auto-focus and zoom control, which are handy when you need them; and most camcorders are designed to be handheld or carried on the shoulder for long periods, so they're comfortable to use.

✔ **Action cameras:** Recent developments in technology have permitted camera manufacturers to fit more into less space. This has led to the introduction of *action cameras,* which are very small, light camcorders that can be strapped to sport equipment, bikes, or cars and can record video that's normally hard to capture. (See Figure 1-5.) For example, a cyclist could attach an action camera to his helmet to record what he sees as he is cycling. Action cameras can also be attached to free runners, skiers, sky divers, and race-car drivers to give the audience a feeling of being involved.

Action cameras are a great, inexpensive way to capture high-quality video. You can expect to pay as little as $50 for an action camera. Note, however, that the sound quality on these cameras isn't the best, which may influence your decision to buy one. Usually, however, action cameras are used for capturing shots in which sound isn't needed or isn't the primary focus.

I've used action cameras to record vehicles as they are driving. In such cases, I've attached the camera either to the windshield inside the car to film the driver or to the outside of the car to capture the car driving on the road.

Figure 1-5

✔ **Aerial cameras:** Shots filmed from the sky can look amazing, and they're now being used more frequently within films and TV programs. Aerial video can be captured by attaching cameras to drones or quadcopters to get stunning wide-shot footage that you couldn't get from the ground.

Before drones and quadcopters were developed, the only way to get footage from the sky was by taking a camera up in a full-size helicopter, an expensive option. Aerial cameras give the same effect for a lot less money.

A number of different types of drones and quadcopters are available from camera stores and most start from around $50.

In some countries, you need a license to fly a drone or quad-copter, so make sure you know what the rules are where you live.

✓ **DSLR video:** For many years, cameras used two lenses — one through which the photograph was captured on film, and another that passed the image to the viewfinder that the photographer would look through. This approach had some problems, however: Sometimes the images photographers thought they were capturing weren't the ones they ended up with later when the photos were developed. The single-lens reflex camera (and later, the digital single-lens reflex camera, or DSLR) changed that: With the single-lens approach, the image you saw through the viewfinder was the same as what you captured on film.

Basically, a DSLR camera is one that uses a mirror behind the lens to reflect what's happening through the lens into the eye piece. The DSLR is a still-photography camera that uses detachable lenses and produces some amazing images. Within the past ten years or so, manufacturers began including a video function with their DSLR cameras that allows you to capture beautiful video, too.

DSLR cameras (see Figure 1-6) are more compact than some of the cinematic cameras, so they're great for capturing video if you're traveling or shooting in small spaces.

DSLR video can look very cinematic, which means it looks more like the quality you would see on a blockbuster film in the cinema. The reasons for this are:

- They are equipped with bigger sensors, which capture more of the scene you are filming — more light, and a greater depth of field. See the nearby sidebar, "Depth of field."

- They allow you to attach different lenses so you can get a variety of shots. A good lens can create a beautiful shot.

For a number of reasons, DSLRs are not great for recording long video clips: They can be complicated to set up, for instance, and because they can overheat, they have a limited recording time. Additionally, recording sound with these devices isn't easy: The onboard microphone is mediocre at best; while recording, the camera produces quite a bit of noise; and the only way to connect an external microphone is through a mini jack.

Figure 1-6

I used DSLR cameras for video when they were first released and I've filmed many short films using them. The video was great, but because of DSLR's limitations with sound, I had to record sound using a separate device and then match the sound to the video later, during the editing process. If you're working on a large project, matching sound like this can take a long time.

✔ **Digital cinema cameras:** Digital cinema cameras (see Figure 1-7) are used to film larger film projects and they give a more cinematic feel and look to the footage. Like camcorders, digital cinema cameras have become more affordable and more compact. Fifty years ago, you would have needed a truck to carry around your cinema camera and equipment, but nowadays they can fit into your rucksack.

Digital cinema cameras can be purchased from most large camera stores and range in price from $1,000 to more than $60,000.

Digital cinema cameras are usually larger than most cameras because they have more technology to fit into the inside of the

Figure 1-7

camera body. They are also usually the more expensive option: With digital cinema cameras, you buy the body of the camera only and then add additional attachments, including lenses and monitors, later. Some of these attachments cost as much as the camera body.

As with DSLRs, cinema cameras have larger sensors inside the camera body to capture more light and more depth of field.

Cinema cameras tend to have more manual settings and can be complicated to set up. Because of this, I mainly use my cinema camera for dramas and films (and sometimes for corporate projects). On film projects, I have more time to change lenses and adjust settings to get the shot I want.

Depth of field

Depth of field is the area around your subject that is in focus. A shot that has a shallow depth of field has a smaller area in focus around your subject. This produces a blurred background that can make your shot look cinematic. As you can see the figure, the subject, Paige, is in focus, but the background is blurry and out of focus.

A shot that has a wider depth of field, on the other hand, has a larger area in focus around your subject. This is better if you want to get more of your scene in focus or if you have a lot of movement in your shot and you don't want your subject to go out of focus. An example of a wide depth of field appears in the figure below. As you can see, in this figure, Paige is in focus and the background is also in focus.

To have more control over the depth of field in your shots, your choice of camera is important. If you want to create a shallow depth of field within your shots, choose a cinema camera or a DSLR with a large sensor.

How to Record and Import Footage

You may be wondering why I've included a section on recording and importing footage here — you just press Record, right? It's not quite as simple as that. Many mistakes have been made at this stage, including mine: I set up the camera and was so busy watching my actors' Oscar-winning performances onscreen that I failed to notice I hadn't pressed Record — it's easily done!

Take your time. It's important not to rush when setting up your camera. Rushing can lead to mistakes. I prefer to make sure everything is set up before I call my actors in. If they arrive early, I get them to read through their lines and prepare for the shot, which gives me more time to set the shot up and make sure everything is ready before I start filming.

Directors often give instructions to cast and crew as part of the filming routine. If you watch behind-the-scenes footage from films, you can sometimes hear the directors calling out instructions to the team. (See Figure 1-8.) These may seem like code if you don't know what they mean. The following list describes some of the most common:

Figure 1-8

✔ **"Quiet on set":** This grabs the attention of the crew and actors around and warns them you are filming and that everyone should stop talking. If people continue to talk, you may need to shout louder.

✔ **"Roll sound":** This is a cue for the sound operator to start the sound recording (if you're capturing sound separately). It's also an opportunity for him or her to warn you of any unwanted noises. If all is clear and your sound operator has set the sound recording, he will respond with "Sound rolling" or just give you a thumbs-up. (See Figure 1-9.)

Figure 1-9

✔ **"Roll camera":** This is a cue for the camera operator to start the camera recording. When she's done this, she'll respond with "Camera rolling." Remember to keep your finger away from the Record button while filming — you may accidentally press it again and stop recording. (See Figure 1-10.)

Figure 1-10

If you watch behind-the-scenes documentaries about the making of films you see the camera operator shout out "speed" instead of "rolling." This is a leftover from the days when the cameras recorded onto reels of tape. On those cameras, the motors inside the cameras would need a few seconds to get the reel of tape rolling at the right speed. Back then, the camera operator would wait until the camera was rolling at the right speed and would shout "speed" to let the director know it was okay to record. This term may be out-of-fashion, but some camera operators still use it. You can use either "speed" or "rolling"; it's up to you.

✏ **"Slates":** This is the cue for the person with the clapperboard to introduce the scene and take number. (See the nearby sidebar, "Using a clapperboard.") (See Figure 1-11.)

Figure 1-11

✔ **"Action":** This is the last instruction to be called before the scene begins. It instructs the actors to start acting. (See Figure 1-12.)

Figure 1-12

✔ **"Cut":** This instructs the camera and sound operator to stop recording after the actors have finished the scene. It's important not to shout this too early: You may need the extra video footage later, when you're editing your film.

After many of the instructions called by the director, the crew is expected to respond — to confirm, for instance, that the sound

Using a clapperboard

You may be wondering why a clapperboard is used in filmmaking. A clapperboard is used when you record video and sound separately, usually on bigger film productions. Details of the film and scene will be written on the clapperboard so it's easier to organize when editing. In the past, the information was written onto the clapperboard in chalk, but these days marker pens are used. When the operator stands in front of the camera and claps the clapperboard, the sound recorded and the video of it closing can be synced together when editing (if you're recording sound separately).

and camera are rolling. Even if I'm filming on my own, I tend to call out the instructions as a reminder to myself and also to let people around me know that I am filming. It's good to get into this habit for when you work with a larger film crew.

Importing your footage from your camera can be done in two ways, as explained below:

↳ **Importing directly from the camera:** This involves connecting your digital video camera to the computer directly via a USB or FireWire cable. Your camera instructions will be able to show you where the USB or FireWire connection is on your camera. (See Figure 1-13.)

Your editing tool should recognize when the camera is connected and you can import your footage from the camera.

This will be covered in more detail in Project 5 as you import and edit footage from your camera.

Figure 1-13

✔ **Importing from the media card:** This involves removing the media card from the camera and inserting it into a media card reader connected to your computer. (See Figure 1-14.)

Your editing tool should recognize the media card when it's inserted and you will be able to import the video clips from your media card.

I use this method because I always remove the media cards after filming to make sure I don't record over them or lose them. Some film projects require many media cards so I put them into a case and name them, which makes it easier to sort through footage when editing.

Figure 1-14

Try It Out Yourself

Now that you're armed with some knowledge about the different types of cameras available, and a basic understanding of how to record and import footage, it's time to get to know your camera in the best way possible — by getting out there and recording with it. Don't film anything too complicated to begin with; try filming things around the house or in your garden or local park. This will help you get familiar with the functions and features on your camera so you'll be ready when you begin shooting your first film project.

Framing a Great Shot

Taking time to frame the shots in your film is one of the most important things you can do to improve the look of your film. It can take your film from looking like a home video to looking more like an award-winning movie.

Framing a shot refers to the way you position your camera with respect to the subject. By framing a shot, you choose what you see through the viewfinder on your camera and what your audience will see when they watch your film. There are many different ways to frame a shot and many different types of shots you can use to help make your film look great.

You can use framing to make a character or object stand out, to express emotion, to make your characters look more or less important, and to affect the way your audience feels when watching your film. You can also change angles and change how much information is in the frame during a scene to keep your's audience attention.

In this project, I show you how to make your shots look great, and you'll have the opportunity to frame different types of shots using your own camera.

Learning the Rule of Thirds

Framing a shot is not just about pointing a camera at a subject and pressing a button. You should take time to consider the best way to frame your shot — *every* shot — because doing so will always pay off in the final edit.

The *rule of thirds* is one of the most basic and important rules to remember when shooting your film. It's not really a "rule" in the strict sense, and you won't be arrested for not using it, but it does make your shots look better.

The rule of thirds was first used in paintings and photography and then later in film and TV. Instead of placing subjects in the middle of the frame, artists, photographers, and filmmakers use the rule of thirds to position their subjects and actors to make the shot look more interesting. Let me show you how it works.

Each of the images in Figure 2-1 is an identical shot of one of our actors. I have divided the second frame into thirds, horizontally and vertically: three sections across and three sections down. This is where we get rule of *thirds* from.

When I filmed this shot I wanted to draw attention to the actor's eyes, so I framed the shot with the eyes two-thirds of the way up the frame and two-thirds of the way across the frame.

Figure 2-1

This leaves my actor positioned more to the right of the frame. I could have moved her more to the left instead, but because the actor is already looking to the left of the frame, positioning to the right is the preferred choice. It's better to leave some open space for the actor to look into. As you can see in Figure 2-2, moving the actor over to the left of the frame looks odd and crowded, and may distract the audience.

Figure 2-2

Using the rule of thirds is like riding a bike: It takes practice. If you use the rule often enough, framing shots this way will become natural to you, and you'll be able to do it without thinking about it.

Next time you watch a movie, look out for the ways the director uses the rule of thirds. Sometimes you can spot moments in films where the director intentionally breaks the rule of thirds to make the shot feel awkward. (Just make sure you spot these moments quietly. Constantly pointing out awkward shots may annoy your family or friends. For this reason, some people now refuse to watch films with me.)

Choosing the Right Shot

The beauty of filmmaking is that you can move your camera around and change your shot types throughout a scene. When the audience can see a whole scene — from a wide shot to the close-ups that show the characters' facial expressions and emotions — they get immersed into the scene and have a more engaging experience.

Choosing the right type of shots for your film can enhance a scene's look and build emotions and mood. Be sure to take time in choosing your shots, then, before filming begins. Some filmmakers prefer to plan their shots very early, during the planning stage. Others prefer to choose shots in the storyboarding phase, which comes after writing the script. Choosing your shots in advance helps save time on the day of filming because the director and crew are prepared and know what shots to set up, light, and capture.

Despite the advantages of choosing shots ahead of time, some filmmakers like to choose their shots on the day of filming, when the set, props, costumes, and actors are all assembled and ready to go, which helps them to decide on what shots to use. I prefer to mixed approach: I like to prepare my shots when storyboarding, but I often change at least some of these shots (or add new shots) when filming as I find better ways of framing the shot or as a new angle I didn't anticipate becomes clear to me.

In this section, I explain about the different types of shots you can use in your scenes, how they can help to tell the story, and when to use them.

Shooting a wide shot

A *wide shot,* also known as a *long shot,* shows your audience more of the scene you are filming. You do this by zooming out on your camera or by simply moving your camera farther away from your subject or character. Figure 2-3 shows a wide shot; next to it is the same shot with a grid superimposed on it so you can see how it was framed using the rule of thirds. As you can see, I framed our actor's head in the top left.

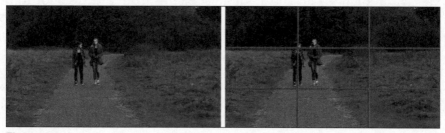

Figure 2-3

Some filmmakers like to start their scenes with a wide shot. When a wide shot is used this way, it's called an *establishing shot,* and is used to show more of the location surrounding the subject or characters in your scene. Imagine you're filming a scene, and you want your audience to know that your characters are on a beach. One way to do this is to begin the scene with a wide shot showing your characters, the sky, the sea, and the sand. Instantly your audience knows the characters are on a beach.

When framing a shot, look out for any straight lines you can find, either horizontally or vertically across the shot. Use these lines to keep your framing straight. In Figure 2-3, for instance, the shot is framed so that the horizontal line of the shot follows the line where the grass meets the trees.

An *extreme wide shot* is filmed even farther away from your subject or character — in fact, sometimes they're not even visible in the shot. This shot is great for introducing the location of your scene. Figure 2-4 shows an extreme wide shot of the same scene filmed in Figure 2-3.

Figure 2-4

Often blockbuster movies establish the location of a scene by using an extreme wide shot that includes landmarks, buildings, or sights that the audience will recognize.

Shooting a mid shot

The *mid shot* or *medium shot* frames the characters from a space above their heads to a point roughly midway down their bodies. This shot is the most commonly used shot on TV and film because it's great for capturing hand movements, gestures, and facial expressions. Figure 2-5 shows a mid shot taken from a DVD series.

Figure 2-5

The mid shot is used a lot in news reports because it focuses the audience's attention on the upper-half of the bodies of your characters. Because the viewpoint of a mid shot is similar to your own viewpoint when you're having a conversation with someone, it's also the most natural-looking shot for an audience to watch. It's a great shot to use for conversations and dialogue with small groups of people.

A *two shot* is a mid shot used to film two characters together, as shown in Figure 2-6.

Figure 2-6

A two shot is often used in TV when two presenters host a show. It can be used when you have two characters side by side sitting together or walking, or when they're face to face at a dinner table or having coffee.

Over-the-shoulder shots are great for conversations between characters who are facing each other. With an over-the-shoulder shot, you see both characters at the same time but only one character faces the camera, as shown in Figure 2-7.

Figure 2-7

I like to use over-the-shoulder shots because they allow you to see the expressions on a character's face. Because the character faces the viewer, over-the-shoulder shots can make the audience feel like they're in the conversation.

Over-the-shoulder shots also can be used within close-up shots to capture more expression from your character and to build emotion, as in Figure 2-8. (For more on close-up shots, see the next section, "Shooting a close-up shot.")

Figure 2-8

With over-the-shoulder shots, it's common for actors to look at the camera during filming because the camera is very close to the shoulder of the second actor. Actors looking at the camera can be distracting to the audience and could lose any emotion built up in the scene. See an example of this in Figure 2-9. One way to keep your actors from looking at the lens of the camera is to move the camera farther back away from the actor and then zoom in.

Shooting a close-up shot

Bringing the camera closer or zooming into your subject or character creates a *close-up shot,* like the one shown in Figure 2-10.

A close-up shot is a great way to show a character's facial expressions, which can help build emotions in your film. Directors normally use close-ups in scenes to show how a character is feeling. This degree of detail is hard to get with a wide shot or mid shot.

Figure 2-9

Figure 2-10

Because close-up shots convey so much detail on the actor's face, these shots can allow actors to express subtle emotions. Figure 2-11 are images taken from one of the films I acted in. Can you guess which emotions I'm performing?

Figure 2-11

An *extreme close-up shot* comes in even closer to your character or subject to show an even greater degree of strong emotions or fine detail on a subject. If you want your audience to know that your character is really angry, say, you could use an extreme close-up of the actor's face to show the anger in her eyes, as shown in Figure 2-12.

Figure 2-12

You can use an extreme close-up for any shot that requires a lot of detail. For example, if you want to show the object that your character has in his hand, you could use a cut-in to an extreme close-up shot of that object. A *cut-in* is a close-up shot used to show detail on an object or on a part of the subject already visible in the main scene — a close-up, say, of an actor's hands or of the object an actor is holding. See Figure 2-13, which shows a cut-in shot of one character passing over a key to another. In this scene, it is important that the audience see the key being passed from one character to another.

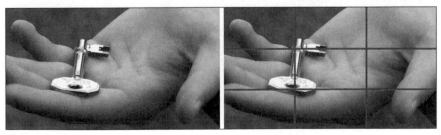

Figure 2-13

Choosing a Fixed-Camera Position or a Moving Camera

Your choice whether to use a fixed camera position or a moving camera depends on the feel, mood, and emotion you want to create in the shot. It's amazing what a small amount of movement from the camera can do to a shot.

What I love about the art of film is that you can use all these different types of shots within a scene. An audience in a theater can only watch a stage performance from one angle, usually from a position too far away to read the actors' facial expressions. (This is why stage actors use big actions and gestures.) With film, however, you can combine any number of shots — start with a wide shot, move in to a mid shot for the dialogue, and then zoom in for a close-up shot — to show even the most subtle expressions and emotions.

In this section, I explain the different styles of filming and describe the ways these styles can enhance the look of your shots and add mood and emotion.

Steady does it! Using a tripod

A tripod is a great tool for keeping your shots steady and for taking the weight of the camera off of your camera operator. (See Figure 2-14.) It's also great for adding subtle or gentle movement to your shots.

Filming a whole movie with a handheld camera can be uncomfortable for the camera operator, so before you choose this approach, be sure that it matches the style and mood of your film. Some films have used the handheld camera technique throughout, but that style was used to add a tense, scary, or point-of-view feel to the shots. I explain this in more detail later in this chapter in the section, "Adding drama with handheld shots."

Figure 2-14

I like to film some of my shots on a tripod and some handheld because this can change the mood and feeling through the scenes. It depends on what feeling I want the scene to have. If I want to give a calm or relaxed feel to the scene, or if I want the audience to focus on the performance of my actors, I use a tripod.

With a tripod, you can also add movement to your shots to make them more interesting, as follows:

✔ **Pan shot:** A *pan shot* is achieved by moving your camera on a tripod from right to left or from left to right (depending on what is happening in your scene) while filming. Figure 2-15 shows our crew filming a shot of two actors walking on a path. The camera turns to follow the actors as they walk from right to left.

Montrose Reg. Library Dist.
320 S. 2nd St.
Montrose, CO 81401

It's best to avoid too much panning within one shot because this could disorient the audience or make them feel uncomfortable. I would aim to keep to one panning movement per shot, if needed.

Figure 2-15

You can see examples of pan shots on the *Digital Filmmaking For Kids For Dummies* companion site.

✔ **Tilt shot:** A *tilt shot* is achieved by moving your camera vertically on a tripod, from pointing up to pointing down or vice versa, depending on what you're filming. Figure 2-16 shows our crew filming an establishing shot of a scene. In this shot, the camera operator tilts the camera down from the top of the trees to the characters talking together on the path.

You can see examples of tilt shots on the *Digital Filmmaking For Kids For Dummies* companion site.

Figure 2-16

Adding drama with handheld shots

By simply holding the camera to film your scenes, you can add drama and emotion to your shots. This means that your footage can look more interesting and a bit more exciting.

When using the handheld technique, it's important to hold the camera with both hands when filming. This supports the camera and reduces some of the shaking from your hands. Don't worry, the shots will still look dramatic. When filming handheld shots, I like to place one hand in the camera's hand strap and one underneath the camera, as shown in Figure 2-17.

If I'm filming a high action scene or if I want to add energy to my shots, I prefer to shoot handheld. Handheld shots are used often in chase scenes and fight scenes to make the scene look more chaotic and realistic and to grab the attention of the audience. It can also make the audience feel as if they are looking through the eyes of your character. Such shots are called *point-of-view (POV) shots*.

Figure 2-17

Using a camera stabilizer

A *camera stabilizer* combines the look and feel of handheld and tripod shots and creates beautifully smooth shots. The original camera stabilizer, the Steadicam, was invented by a camera operator called Garrett Brown and was first introduced in 1975. Camera stabilizers are great for following actors or subjects through a scene without having to cut and change angle or move the tripod. The shots from a camera stabilizer are so smooth that it gives the impression that the camera is flying. The shots within films that use camera stabilizers to shoot long, sweeping, and continuous shots look amazing.

Steadicams can be expensive to buy, but alternative versions for smaller cameras are available at camera stores from around $25. Or check out the YouTube videos that show you how to make your own camera stabilizer.

Try It Out Yourself

So, it's time to grab your camera again. This time try filming the different types of shots, including a wide shot, mid shot, and close-up shot. You don't have to film any dialogue or any acting yet: As before, you can just film things in your garden, your park, or around your house. (Consider filming your pet!) You'll edit the shots you film later, in Project 5. Remember, the best way to develop your skills as a filmmaker is to get out there and shoot.

Making Your Film Sound Good

To your audience, the quality of your film's sound is as important as the quality of the picture. Poor sound can be distracting and deflect your audience's attention away from your story.

To record sound when filming, you must use a microphone. A *microphone* is a device that recognizes noises and sounds and converts the sound into data and information that is recorded onto the media card with the video footage from your camera. You can either use the microphone built into the camera or plug an external microphone into your camera.

When filming, it's important you spend as much time getting your movie's sound right as you do getting its picture right. When it all comes together, your film may turn out twice as good.

By taking the time to record good sound you'll save time editing the film later. Fixing badly recorded sound in an editing tool is very difficult and in some cases impossible. If the sound is poorly recorded or if there is a noise that is impossible to remove, the sound often must be re-recorded and replaced in the editing tool. I have had to do this a few times due to noises that I didn't notice when filming. It's very hard to re-record dialogue because you have to get the actors to say the lines in the same way as they did during the original filming so that their filmed mouth movements fit the re-recorded audio. This is why it's best to try and get it right when filming.

For mainstream movies, the sound is recorded separately using very expensive equipment and then synced together with the picture later during editing. Don't worry if you don't have this equipment; in this chapter, I show you simple ways to make your film sound good using the your camera's microphone or an external microphone.

Using Your Camera's Built-In Microphone

Nearly all digital camcorders now have built-in microphones called *onboard microphones*. (See Figure 3-1.) On the latest cameras, onboard microphones are better than they used to be but they're still not the best solution for recording audio or dialogue in film. Still, at the moment an onboard microphone may be your only solution, so in this section I explain how to get the best results from the on-board microphone on your camera.

Figure 3-1

Onboard microphones can be useful for some projects where you may not have room for an external microphone or boom pole. A few years ago, I filmed a documentary in Ghana and all I took with me was a camcorder and a camera-mounted microphone. Because I was the only member of the film crew, I couldn't use an external boom microphone, and I had to fit all my filming equipment in my carry-on luggage on the plane. It was a challenging experience, but it taught me a lot about recording with onboard microphones. Recording sound with a camera-mounted microphone isn't easy, but try using the following techniques to get the best sound:

- **Get close:** To get the highest quality sound, try to get your microphone as close to your subject or character as possible. Sometimes this isn't easy, especially if you are shooting a wide shot, but you may be able to use the sound recorded in the close-up shot or mid shot from the same scene. Having a microphone built into the camera makes it even harder than usual to get the microphone as close as possible to your subject, and you may have to ask your actors to speak clearly and to project their voices. Another option is to turn the level of the microphone on your camera up, but this only increases the overall volume, including background noise.

✔ **Reduce camera noise:** With onboard-sound recording, you're more likely to record noise from the camera itself. Such noise may be from the electronics inside the camera, especially when zooming in and out, or it may come from the sounds you make when pressing buttons or handling the camera while recording. The best way to avoid these noises is to try not to move your hands too much or press buttons when recording. Mounting your camera on a tripod ensures you don't have to hold or touch the camera as it's recording, which helps to reduce any noises made by your hands.

✔ **Reduce background noise:** It's not easy to control the noises around you when you're filming, especially if you're filming in a public place, such as a park or street. Big-movie film directors can afford to close roads and public places to control noise, but you won't be able to. Onboard microphones tend to pick up background noises even more often than external microphones, so it's important to try and reduce the amount of noise around you when filming to make it easier for your audience to hear your actors. Before you start filming, ask your cast and crew to be quiet for a few minutes so you can detect any background noises that may cause problems when recording.

To avoid unwanted background noises when filming, ask your crew to keep quiet. Microphones can be very sensitive and may pick up noises that you may not hear. You'll only notice these noises when you import your footage at the editing stage. Ask your crew to keep still, too, because even gentle footsteps may be picked up by the microphone.

Recording with External Microphones

Recording sound with an external microphone can produce better results than using an onboard microphone because it allows you to place your camera in one position and then record sound from a position that's closer to your subject or character. This also helps reduce unwanted background noise.

To use an external microphone when filming, have an extra crew member hold the microphone and monitor the sound during filming. This extra crew member is called the *sound operator* or *boom operator*.

The external microphone is normally attached to a *boom pole,* which allows the sound operator to get the microphone closer to the subject or actor without appearing in the shot himself. Your boom operator should be able to hold the boom pole for long periods without dropping it. If the boom operator's arm gets tired of holding the weight of the microphone and boom, the microphone could appear in the shot. (See Figure 3-2.)

Figure 3-2

Some video cameras have a socket on the camera body — either a mini jack or an XLR socket — into which you can plug an external microphone. Figure 3-3 shows you what each of these sockets looks like.

Figure 3-3

When recording with an external microphone, try using the following techniques to get the best sound:

✔ **Point the microphone in the direction of the sound:** External microphones are normally directional microphones, which means they pick up sound directly in front of the microphone and not to the sides or behind it. This is good because it will record more sounds from the subject and less noise from around the subject. (See Figure 3-4.)

With external microphones, it's important to point the microphone where the sound is coming from. If the microphone is pointing away from the action, it won't record the sound you want. The dialogue will sound quiet and muffled, and you'll have more background noise.

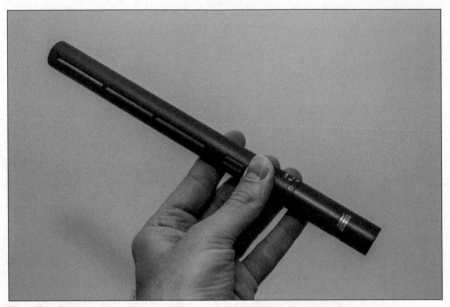

Figure 3-4

✓ **Position the external microphone appropriately:** When recording sound with an external microphone, you have two options. You can position the microphone above your subject or below it. The best choice of position can depend on what you are filming:

- *Overhead:* Suspending the microphone over the scene is the most common approach. Overhead microphones are better for wider shots because they make it less likely that the microphone will appear in your shot.

  Overhead shots also offer better sound from your actors and avoid noises made from your actors' hands or feet.

  Figure 3-5 shows a member of our film crew recording sound using the overhead technique.

- *Underneath:* Recording sound from underneath is mainly used when filming mid shots or close-up shots.

Figure 3-5

This option can be used if you have limited room above the actors or if you want to shield the microphone from high winds outside.

Figure 3-6 shows a member of our film crew recording sound using the underneath technique.

Ask your boom operator to keep his or her hands still when holding the boom during filming because any tapping or movement of the hands on the boom pole may be picked up by the microphone and distract from the dialogue being recorded.

Figure 3-6

✔ **Avoid dropping the boom in the shot:** A boom pole with an external microphone on the end can feel heavy, especially if you have to hold it during a long scene. Sometimes the microphone can drop down into the shot, which means filming will have to be stopped. (See Figure 3-7.) It's important to look out for this because the boom can sometimes just creep into a shot, which you may overlook until you import your footage onto your computer later.

Figure 3-7

To help avoid the microphone appearing in your shots, I suggest asking your boom operator to rest between takes. When you're not filming, the operator can simply put the boom pole down on the floor — the lower end of the pole, that is, not the end with the microphone, because otherwise he or she may damage the microphone.

Recording Sound Separately

There are times when a filmmaker needs to record sound using a separate device from the camera, to record sound separately and then sync the sound to the video later, when editing. Usually, the reason for this is to increase the quality of the recorded sound because many cameras don't record sound as well as external recorders can. Another reason is so that the sound operator can move farther away from the camera and still monitor the sound being recorded. (Usually, of course, the sound operator has to be close to the camera in order to monitor the sound being recorded.)

When recording sound separately, you should try to make it as easy as possible to sync the picture and audio later in the editing tool. There are two basic ways to do this:

- ✓ **Use a clapperboard:** A clapperboard is often used when making films to display information about the scene being shot — the scene number, take number, crew details, and so on. It's also used to sync video and sound. When the clapperboard is snapped closed in front of the camera, it creates a visual cue on the video footage, whose sound creates an audio marker point that can be used to sync with the video when editing.

✓ **Record sound from both the camera and the external microphone:** When recording sound on an external device, I always capture sound through the camera, too. I use this sound only as a reference, though, and not as sound in the final edit. When recording sound through the camera you pick up dialogue, which can be used to sync the externally recorded sound to in the editing tool. This saves a huge amount of time trying to read people's lips to sync the sound when editing.

When I record sound separately from the camera, I prefer to use a device called a portable sound recorder. Portable sound recorders can be purchased from camera stores from around $100 to around $10,000. My favorite is the Zoom H4N (see Figure 3-8).

Figure 3-8

The Zoom H4N is an amazing little device that records great quality sound. It's really portable and is a lot less expensive than most other portable sound recorders.

The great thing about portable sound recorders is that you can use them to record sound effects or voiceovers without having to set up your camera. I often use my portable sound recorder to record *foley* or *wildtrack,* which are background sounds that can be added to the film during editing. Foley or wildtrack sound fills out the sound in a scene and enhances the audience's experience. For example, if you are filming a party scene and you want to make it sound like there are loads of people at the party, you could film the scene with the actors you have and then record sounds of people talking and laughing and any other background noises from a real party you attend and then add these noises to the video when editing.

Try It Out Yourself

Now it's your turn. Try recording audio through your camera using the techniques described here. You don't need to worry about preparing a scene to film; you can just record sounds around the house or in your neighborhood. Recording good-quality sound is good preparation for your first film project.

Getting the Best Lighting

Light is important to your film. Without light, your audience won't be able to see your actors. Light can also be used to help create the mood of your shots or to affect the feelings and emotions of your audience.

Video cameras need light more than our eyes do. Our eyes are sensitive to light and can adjust to light and dark very quickly. If you walk from a dark room into the sunshine outside, for example, your eyes usually adjust to the change in light so quickly you don't notice. Cameras also have a feature that adjusts to different light, but it's not as good as the one in our eyes. This is why most film productions use extra lights to help light the actors.

In blockbuster films, crews use very powerful lights to act as sunlight or moonlight because natural light can be unpredictable and unreliable. Natural light would make scenes shot over the course of a few days look inconsistently lit, with, say, bright sunshine on the first day of filming and overcast light on the next. Even when a scene is shot indoors, TV and film crews will build their sets inside a studio and place lights outside the window to simulate sunlight or moonlight.

In mainstream films, *lighting technicians* and *gaffers* are responsible for designing and setting up the lighting for each scene. They work with the director and the camera operator to determine where and how much lighting is needed for a scene.

There are many different types and strengths of lights available to use on your film. In this chapter, I show you how to use light to make your films look great.

Using Natural Light

Buying lights for filming can be expensive, but don't worry, you have one of the biggest and most powerful lights available for you to use for free — the sun! Sunlight or daylight is a great source of light, but it's only available during the day. (See Figure 4-1.)

When you're filming outside during the day, the light from the sun will light your actor. If there are a few or no clouds in the sky, you will have direct sunlight, and you may see more shadows around your subject or actor. You may also find you get shadows on the actor's face. (See Figure 4-2.)

With direct sunlight it's hard to avoid shadows unless you point the actor directly into the sun, but bright sunlight can make her squint her eyes, which is probably not a good look for your actor. (See Figure 4-3.)

Figure 4-1

Figure 4-2

You can remove some of the shadows by using a reflector to bounce the light back into the darker areas of the your subject or actor's face. (See Figure 4-4.)

Figure 4-3

Figure 4-4

You can buy reflectors for filming or you could use anything that has a large white surface, such as a polystyrene board or large sheet of white card. By angling the reflector toward your subject or actor, the white surface will reflect the sunlight.

It's important to remember to avoid filming your actor with the sun behind them because this places the light source at the back of the actor's head and not at the face, and will leave the actor backlit and shadowy. (See Figure 4-5.) This can also cause lens flares, which look like circular blobs or streaks of light across your shot. Lens flares can sometimes look great, but they also highlight any dirt or smudges on the lens of your camera.

Lens flares have recently become pretty respectable in main-stream films. Rather than hide lens flares, a number of high-profile films have actually flaunted them. J.J. Abrams, for instance, director and producer of many films, including *Mission: Impossible III* and the recent *Star Trek* and *Star Wars* films, is a huge fan of lens flares. The lens flares in J.J. Abrams's films are added during post-production during the editing process. You can find lens-flare effects in most editing suites, including iMovie, Final Cut, and Adobe Premiere.

Figure 4-5

On a cloudy day you'll have fewer problems with shadows and lens flares because the clouds covering the sunlight act like a filter to disperse light around your scene. This places the light all around your subjects or actors and you'll have fewer shadows.

You can also use daylight to help light scenes in a room as long as you have windows for the daylight to come through. Daylight coming through only one window in a room may add shadows to your subject or actor, but these can be removed by adding extra light inside the room.

Using Extra Lights

When sunlight or daylight is not available, you'll need extra lights to light your subject or actors. (See Figure 4-6.) These can be expensive, but it's also possible to use lights that you already have around the house.

Figure 4-6

Before you go moving lights around your house, please check with an adult first and even ask him or her to help you.

When I first started making films, I didn't have any lights, so I used desk lamps to light my actors. These were great for lighting a close-up shot but usually weren't powerful enough to light a whole scene in a wide shot.

You can also buy low-cost LED lights, which are brilliant. I have some camera-mounted LED lights that run from AA batteries that I use in most productions because they're small, lightweight, and can be used to fill in light to darker areas in a scene or to add more light to a subject. I sometimes even take them with me when I'm filming outside because they can fill shadows on a subject and add light reflection in an actor's eyes.

Halogen utility lights are also really good to use for lighting scenes. These can be bought from hardware stores for a lot less money than professional lighting. If you aren't sure what these look like, try searching for them on the Internet.

Halogen utility lights get hot when in use, so be sure to let them cool down before moving them around. They also use a lot of power so you may want to ask an adult or parent to help set them up.

Extra lights are essential when filming in rooms or other situations without any daylight or sunlight. If your camera is set to automatic and you're filming a scene with low light, your camera will try and boost the brightness of the video and the quality of the picture will decrease. You may end up with a grainy image with lots of dots. (See Figure 4-7.) This can look good in some shots, but it's not an effect you want to achieve accidentally. Even if it's an effect you're looking for, it's best to light your film as well as possible and then add such effects later, when you're editing.

Figure 4-7

Lighting Your Film

Taking time to light your film saves time when editing. If you over-light or under-light your shots, you will have to spend more time in the editing tool adjusting and changing settings to make your footage look better. Trust me, I have spent many hours editing and fixing shots that I have lit badly.

The main thing to remember when lighting your film is to make sure that every shot looks natural. When the scene you see in your viewfinder during filming doesn't look natural, then some-thing is wrong. In the viewfinder, your subject or actor should look as much as possible like it does when you look directly at it without a camera.

Here are some things to consider when lighting your film:

✔ **Overexposed shots:** If your shots are overexposed, it means they are too bright and some of the brighter areas of the image may have gone white and lost detail. Figure 4-8 is an overex-posed shot of one of our actors. You can see that some of the areas of the face have gone completely white and we have lost some of the detail and color. It's difficult (usually impossible) to restore this detail when editing.

Overexposure can be caused by placing too much light on your subject or in your scene, or it can happen because the iris on your camera is open too wide or the aperture is set too low. You can fix this easily by reducing the amount of light entering your scene or by raising the aperture levels.

Figure 4-8

↙ **Underexposed shots:** If your shots are underexposed, this means that they are too dark and you may not be able to see some areas of your subject or actor. Figure 4-9 is the same shot as in Figure 4-8, but it's underexposed instead of overexposed. You can see that there is only part of the face visible in the shot and we have lost some detail in the dark areas. This is easier to repair when editing but it's still not great to have to boost the brightness too much as it can affect the color of your subject and you can end up with a grainy image.

Figure 4-9

✔ **Three-point lighting:** This is a lighting technique used in film and TV that requires three lights set up around the subject or actor. Figure 4-10 shows where the lights are placed in a three-point lighting setup. The three lights are as follows:

- *Key light:* This light can be set up on either side of the subject and it provides the most amount of light to the subject. The key light provides light to one side of the subject's face.

- *Fill light:* This light is positioned on the opposite side to the key light and is used to fill in light to reduce the shadows on the face. This is set a little lower in brightness to the key light.

- *Back light:* This light is positioned behind the subject to one side and provides light to the back of the subject. It may seem like it doesn't do anything but it provides light around the head to separate the subject from the background.

Figure 4-11 shows what each light does on its own. Figure 4-12 shows what all three lights do together.

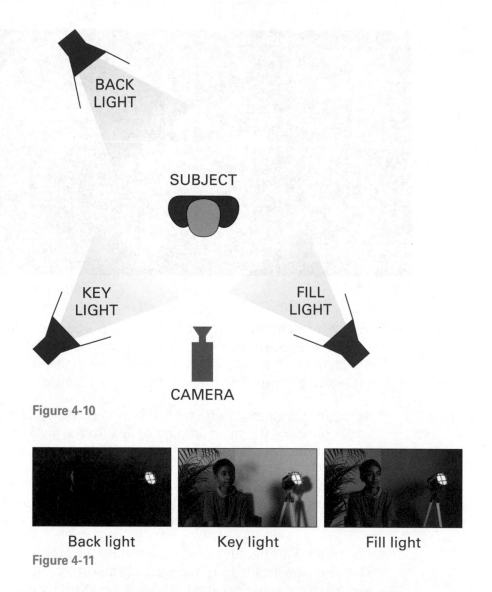

Figure 4-10

| Back light | Key light | Fill light |

Figure 4-11

✔ **Bounced light:** This is my favorite technique because it provides the most natural light to a scene. Bounced lighting involves reflecting light off walls, ceilings, and reflectors onto a subject. (See Figure 4-13.) Sometimes shining a light directly can cast shadows behind a subject or add an unnatural amount of light to a face. Bouncing light off the ceiling, wall, or reflector, however, disperses the light around the room and creates a more natural look for the subject and the shot.

Figure 4-12

Figure 4-13

Occasionally I like to use a mixture of bounced light and direct light to get a reflection of light in an actor's eyes. It can produce a sharper-looking image. Figure 4-14 is a close-up shot of one of our actors with just bounced light.

Figure 4-14

In Figure 4-15, however, we combined a key light with bounced light. Note how the eyes reflect the light.

Figure 4-15

If you don't have many lights in your room, you can reflect light onto your subject using tin foil. You could even wrap it around a cardboard sheet to make your own reflector.

Try It Out Yourself

Light is important to film because it helps your actors to be seen and it can add mood and emotion to a shot. You can use light to improve your own films. Grab your camera and see how it reacts to different amounts of light. Film something in a darker room with low light and then film it again outside during the day. Import the footage and see the difference in quality. If you have extra lights, use them to light a subject. Try bouncing light off the walls to create different lighting effects. Practicing lighting techniques now will help prepare you for lighting your first film project later.

Adding Magic
by Editing

Editing is the icing on the cake. Editing is an important part of the filmmaking process because it brings together all the footage you filmed. And as you edit, you'll get the excitement of seeing all your footage put together, sharpened and adapted for better viewing, and made ready for broadcasting or sharing.

After you capture the footage for your film, you use your chosen editing tool to perform some magic to bring it to life. This *magic* includes activities such as arranging your clips, adding visual effects, music, and sound effects.

Big blockbuster films have full-time editors, who work solely on a film's edit. They are given the footage by the film crew and will start editing the footage as the rest of the film is being shot. The editing process on these blockbuster films can take months or even years to complete because there is so much footage to work through and so many effects to add to each clip.

Editors never get involved with the pre-production or filming of the movie. He or she only works on the movie after it's been filmed. After the editor has put together a rough edit, the director will sit and watch the film to see how the film looks, and will make changes to the edit if needed.

In this project, I show you how to import the footage you have just captured, cut it together onto a timeline with some cool transitions, and then export it to show your family and friends.

Choosing an Editing Tool

Many editing tools are available, and they are all different in the effects they offer and the way they work. But the basic functions of editing tools are similar. Film editing tools allow you to import footage from your camera or media card, cut and arrange your clips on a timeline, add transitions, and then export what's in your timeline to a final movie. This is the process that I cover in this project.

In this project, I use Apple's iMovie, which is available only for Apple products. If you have an Apple Mac, you can purchase iMovie through the App Store for a small amount of money. If you have a PC, Windows Movie Maker is the standard editing tool. You may have Windows Movie Maker installed on your computer, but if not, you can download it for free as part of the Windows Essentials Bundle.

Although there are other editing tools you can buy that offer more amazing effects and functions, the low cost tools for the Mac and PC offer more than you need to start with.

Figure 5-1 shows the iMovie workspace layout where you will navigate through the functions to build your timeline from your selected clips.

Figure 5-1

You may have access to Final Cut Pro or Adobe Premiere Pro, which are more advanced editing tools used by industry professionals. There is also Adobe Premiere Elements, which less expensive and offers fewer tools and controls than Premiere Pro but has simpler and quicker effect tools and templates. These tools offer additional effects and functions to enhance the look and sound of a film. The following list compares the features of Final Cut Pro and Adobe Premiere Pro:

- **Final Cut Pro:** A video editing software application developed by Apple that uses a magnetic timeline, which means clips can be inserted and moved around the timeline easily without overwriting other clips.

  - I use Final Cut Pro for smaller projects because it is a great tool for editing simply and quickly.

  - It has great some great preset effects that I use for enhancing the picture and sound.

- It is available to purchase through the Apple App Store and it's only available on the Mac.

✔ **Adobe Premiere Pro:** A timeline-based video editing software application created by Adobe. Adobe Premiere is available Adobe's website as a monthly or yearly subscription. It's available on the Mac and PC.

  Adobe Premiere has fewer preset effects and more manual setting controls, which allows you to get the look you want.

  I use Adobe Premiere Pro for bigger and more complicated projects because it is better at coping with larger projects than Final Cut Pro.

Create a New Event

Before you start importing your footage onto your computer, you need to create a new event. An *event* is the way iMovie stores and keeps the footage and the project so you can easily find your clips and timeline the next time you open the program. I film a new project nearly every day of the year. If all my footage was kept in one folder, it would be really difficult for me to find previous projects and clips. You can create a new event to import your footage into by following these steps:

1. **Open Applications and click the iMovie icon to start iMovie.**

   iMovie opens onscreen.

2. **In the iMovie main screen, select New Event from the File menu.**

3. **Type the phrase** Types of Shots **in the Name text box to name the new event.**

   The Types of Shots event now appears in the Libraries list, as shown in Figure 5-2.

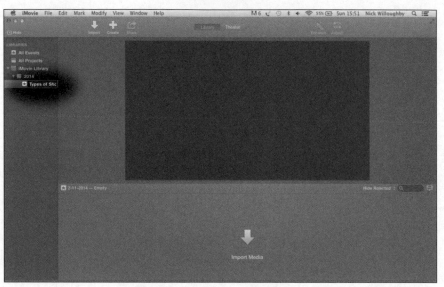

Figure 5-2

Import Your Footage

After you create your event, you can import your footage into it.
When you import footage into iMovie, it stores your video clips in
a folder on your computer's hard drive so you can easily locate
them when editing. Also, after you import your clips, you can disconnect your camera or media card from your computer.

To import your footage, follow these steps:

1. **Connect your camera to your computer with a USB or
   FireWire cable or insert the camera media card into a media
   card reader attached to your computer.**

   The iMovie Import window automatically pops up.

   If the Import window doesn't automatically appear, click the
   Import icon in the toolbar at the upper-left of the workspace.

   Your camera or media card should appear in the Camera/
   Devices pane on the left side of the Import window, as shown
   in Figure 5-3.

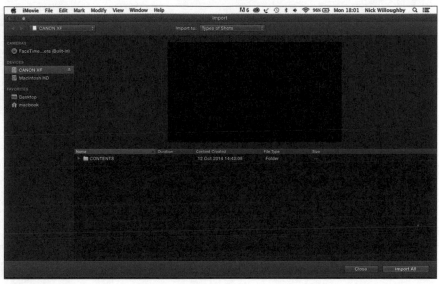

Figure 5-3

2. **Select your card or camera from the Camera/Devices pane.**

   After you select the camera or card, you should see a preview of the first clip recorded in the monitor. Under the monitor is a list of the video clips recorded.

   My camera uses MXF files, Canon's compressed file format, and iMovie won't import these files,. Because MXF files are not recognized by iMovie, I have to use the software that came with the camera to send the video files to my computer, and then convert them before I can finally import them into iMovie. Other editing tools usually don't require this much effort.

3. **In the bottom-right corner of the Import window, click the Import All button. (See Figure 5-4.)**

   As the footage begins importing, a progress circle appears on each clip. These progress circles disappear when your clips have been imported. Do not close the window until all your footage has been imported and all the progress circles have gone.

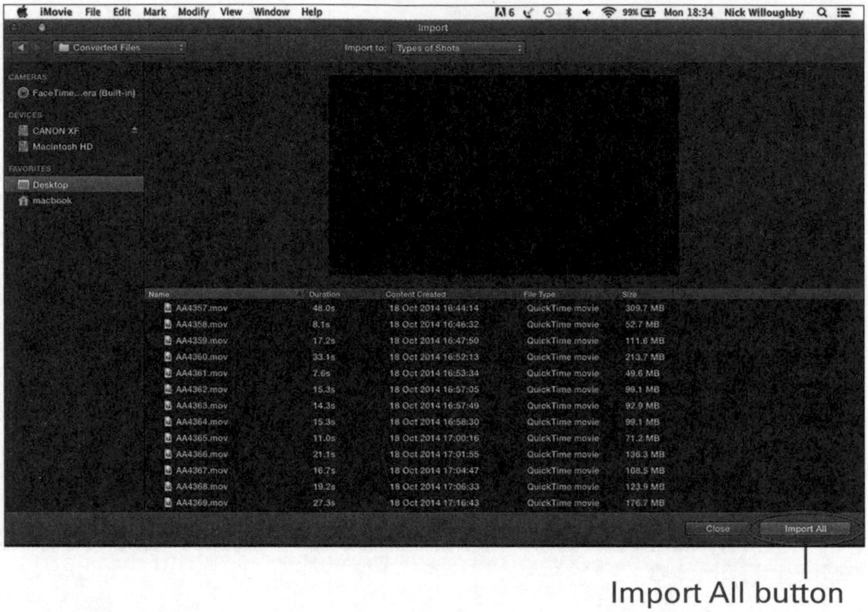

Figure 5-4

After you close the Import window, you see your clips in the event area, as shown in Figure 5-5.

Figure 5-5

4. **Click the red circle in the top-left corner of the screen to close iMovie and get ready to disconnect your camera or media card safely.**

   Don't worry, iMovie automatically saves your project.

5. **Click and hold your camera or media card icon on the desktop, drag it into the trash, and let go.**

   Your camera or media card is safely disconnected.

Create a New Timeline

Your footage is now imported into your event and is ready to be edited. Before you can edit, however, you must create a timeline. A *timeline* or *project* is the area of the editing tool to which you drag your footage to edit and place your clips into the correct sequence in order to build your final film. To create your timeline or project, follow these steps:

1. **Make sure your event is selected, then click Create in the top toolbar and select Movie.**

   A window with a selection of themes opens.

2. **For now, just choose No Theme, and then click the Create button in the bottom-right corner of the Themes window. (See Figure 5-6.)**

   A Create window appears.

3. **In this window, name your project "Types of Shots" and make sure it is being created in the "Types of Shots" event, as shown in Figure 5-7.**

   Your new project now appears above your footage in your event, and the timeline appears below your footage, as shown in Figure 5-8.

Figure 5-6

Figure 5-7

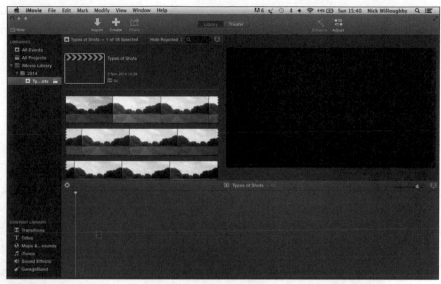

Figure 5-8

Add Selected Footage to a Timeline

With your timeline created, it's now time to add your footage to it. The great thing about iMovie is that you can move clips to your timeline easily and, after they've been added there, you can move them around easily, too. When recording your footage, you'll always have sections at the beginning and the end of the clips that you don't want to keep. These sections normally include extraneous material, such as the director shouting orders at actors, which you probably won't want to include in your film. You can cut off these extraneous bits when you add your footage to your timeline by using the following steps:

1. **Make sure your new project timeline is open.**

2. **Hover the cursor over the first video clip, which should be the wide shot you filmed in Project 2.**

When you hover over the footage, you can see a preview in the Playback Monitor window. Hover the cursor over the part of the clip where you would like to start and then click and drag the cursor to the right. This marks a selection on the clip with a yellow outline. Don't worry if you let go before you've selected everything you'd like to include; you can extend the yellow selected area by clicking on either its left or right edge and dragging to the left or right to lengthen or shorten, as shown in Figure 5-9.

Figure 5-9

3. **Now you have selected the section of your wide shot footage, bring it into the timeline. To do this, click and hold in the center of the selected clip, drag your selection over to the beginning of the timeline, and let go.**

   Your selected clip now appears in the timeline, as shown in Figure 5-10.

4. **View your clips in the timeline to check you have everything you need by hovering your cursor over the Playback Monitor.**

   The playback controls appear, as shown in Figure 5-11.

Figure 5-10

Playback controls

Figure 5-11

Table 5-1 tells you what each playback control does.

Table 5-1	Playback Controls
Control	**What It Does**
[▶]	This button allows you to play the clip you have selected in the timeline.
▶	This plays the footage in the timeline from where your play head is in the timeline. During playback, this turns into the Pause button.
◄◄	This button takes you back to the beginning of the clip. If you hold it down, the clip rewinds during playback.
►►|	This button skips to the next clip in the timeline. If you hold it down, the clip fast forwards during playback.
⤢	This button plays the footage in the timeline in full screen.

When you play your clips, a yellow line moves along the timeline. This line is called the *play head*. You can click and drag the play head along your timeline or move it to a new position by clicking at a point in the area above the clips.

5. **If after playing back you discover you have cut off part of the video at the beginning or end, you can extend the clip in the timeline.**

   To do this, select the clip you would like to extend or shorten and hover over the beginning or end of the clip. The cursor will change to two arrows pointing away from each other. Click and hold, and then move the cursor left or right to shorten or extend the clip.

6. **To add your mid shot clip to the timeline, select the footage you want to include from your mid shot using the same steps you used earlier to add your first clip.**

   When you have selected it, click and drag it to the right of your first clip in the timeline and let go.

This automatically places your mid shot after your wide shot, as shown in Figure 5-12.

Figure 5-12

7. **Repeat this step for the third clip of the close shot and place it to the right of the mid shot clip.**

Table 5-2 lists some keyboard shortcuts that can help with the editing process.

Table 5-2	Keyboard Shortcuts
Keyboard Shortcut	**What It Does**
Command-I	Imports footage into an event
Command-N	Creates new movie project
Command-E	Exports a timeline to the iMovie Theatre
Spacebar	Plays the video in the timeline from where the play head is positioned
Right-arrow key	Moves the play head one frame forward, which can be very useful for precise editing

Keyboard Shortcut	What It Does
Left-arrow key	Moves the play head one frame backward, which can be very useful for precise editing
Down-arrow key	Jumps play head forward to the beginning of the next clip in the event browser or timeline
Up-arrow key	Jumps play head back to beginning of current clip or previous clip in event browser or timeline
Forward slash (/)	Plays the selected area of clip in event browser or timeline
Backslash (\)	Plays from the beginning of the clip, event or timeline
Shift-Command-F	Plays clip from play head position in full screen
Esc	Exits full screen view
Command-Z	To undo last action or change
Shift-Command-Z	To redo last action or change
Command-C	Copies the selected clip or text
Command-X	Cuts the selected clip or text
Command-V	Pastes the copied clip or text

Add Transitions

With your footage in the timeline, the next thing to think about is how one clip joins another, and this is called a *transition*. A transition can be anything from a simple hard cut to a bit of flashy animation, depending on the type of film you're creating. iMovie offers preset transitions, which can be added as follows:

1. **Choose Transitions from the Content Library choices at the bottom left of the iMovie workspace, as shown in Figure 5-13.**

Figure 5-13

2. **Add a fade from black to the beginning of the first clip. To do so, click and hold the Fade to Black transition, drag it over to the beginning of your first clip in the timeline, and let go.**

   A transition icon (shown in Figure 5-14) now appears before your first clip.

   You can now test this transition by selecting the first clip and clicking the Play Clip button in the Playback Monitor window.

3. **Add a crossfade or cross-dissolve between the wide shot and mid shot. To do so, click and hold the Cross Dissolve transition, drag it between the first and second clips in the timeline, and let go.**

   The transition icon now appears between the two clips.

4. **Choose a different transition and add it between the mid shot and close-up clips using the same process.**

Transition icon
Figure 5-14

5. **Finally, add a fade to black to the end of the close-up clip. To do so, click and hold the Fade to Black transition, drag it to the end of the last clip on the timeline, and let go.**

You can see what this all looks like by moving the play head to the beginning of the timeline and clicking the Play button in the Playback Monitor.

Too many transitions!

Try to use transitions carefully because using too many can make your film feel long and not professional. Transitions are usually used to indicate the passage of time or to help change the mood in the story. Using crazy animated transitions such as Mosaic or Spin Out can distract your audience from your story, which is not a good idea. It's best to keep it simple. In films and television shows, you generally only see a few types of transitions, and these tend to be fades and cuts.

Export Your Video

Now that you have put together your three clips in your timeline and added transitions, it's time to save your video by exporting it to share with your friends and family.

Before a video can be viewed by your audience on DVD or a computer, it must be processed and saved by the editing tool. This involves applying the effects to each frame and processing the footage on the timeline as a single video file.

Exporting a video can take a while depending on how long the video is and how many effects you have added to your clips. You can export your video to a file by following these steps:

1. **Make sure your project timeline is open and click on File, then hover over Share and choose File. . . from the drop-down menu. (See Figure 5-15.)**

   The File window appears, and your project's name should appear in the first textbox. (See Figure 5-16.)

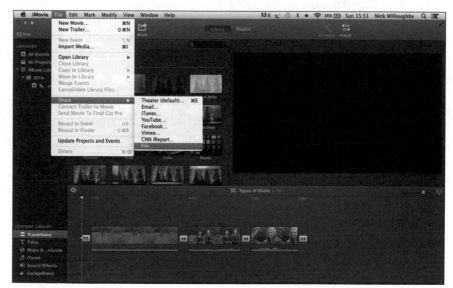

Figure 5-15

2. **Click Next.**

   A small, unnamed window appears, showing you what your file will be called and where it will be saved. (See Figure 5-16.)

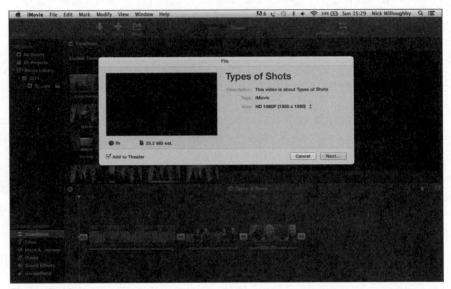

Figure 5-16

3. **Change the file's name and save location, if you want, or leave them as they are. Click Save. (See Figure 5-17.)**

   After your video has been exported, a "Share Successful" notification appears in the top right of the screen. You can now either upload your video to YouTube or play it back for your family and friends. (I show you how to upload to YouTube in the next chapter.)

   You've created an event, imported your footage, placed your clips in the timeline with some transitions, and shared your movie project. Now it's time to move to your first film project.

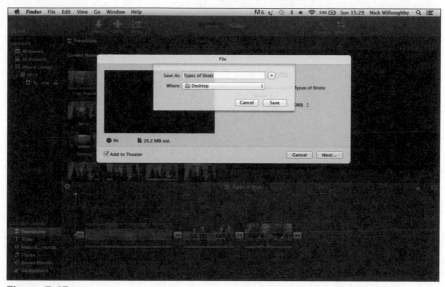

Figure 5-17

Week 2
Making a 60-Second Film Trailer

This week you'll. . .

Ready to take digital filmmaking skills to the next level? At www.dummies.com/extras/digitalfilmmakingforkids, you can view the trailer that our young film crew made. You can also find videos in which I share shooting tips and show you the different types of shots you can use.

Planning Your Film Trailer

A good film trailer is short, *emotive* (that is, it builds emotions and feelings), and leaves the audience wanting more. A film trailer needs to introduce a few basic facts about the film — its genre, the basic story, and any significant details about the characters — to the audience in a very short space of time, and it needs to do this in a way that's interesting and creative in order to motivate the audience to watch the full version of the film.

Film trailers are normally created after the film has been shot, but you will be filming your trailer first. Sometimes filmmakers create a trailer to build interest in their film before it's even made. Creating a trailer before the full film is a great way to see how the story and characters work together. Making your trailer first will give you ideas for the story of the full-version of your film, as well as help you choose what to include and what not to include. To get to the point of filming your trailer, however, you first need to do some planning and preparation.

When creating your film trailer, you need to think about the full version of the film. You may not have developed the story yet but imagine you are presenting your idea to someone who will fund the making of the full version if your film. What will captivate them? How do you introduce your characters? How do you get the story across without giving too much away? Think about a trailer you've seen recently: What was good about it? Watch it again carefully. Try to see what the makers of that trailer did to advertise the full version of the movie.

The planning and writing stage is one of my favorite stages in the filmmaking process. It's a chance to use your creative skills to come up with ideas, create characters, and develop the story.

In this chapter, I show you how to plan and create a great film trailer.

Come Up with an Idea

Coming up with an idea can be one of the hardest parts of filmmaking, but it can be the most exciting, too. I've spent days, weeks, and months thinking of ideas for films and videos. Sometimes I can be driving my car or washing the dishes and an idea just pops into my head.

When thinking about making a film trailer, it's important to decide on the genre of your film. What do I mean by the term *genre?* A *genre* is the type, style, or category of film.

The following list describes most of the main film genres:

- **Action:** Usually a big-budget film that uses high energy, excitement, stunts, chases, explosions, fights, and larger-than-life heroes to tell the story. Examples of action films include *The Maze Runner, Jurassic World,* and *The Dark Knight Rises.*

- **Animated:** A film made from a series of illustrations or drawings to tell the story. Actors' voices are recorded separately for the animated characters' voices. Examples of animated movies include *Frozen, Despicable Me,* and the *Toy Story* films.

- **Adventure:** An adventure film is similar to an action film, but it focuses more on an exciting story than on stunts and explosions. Adventure films often involve a journey. Example of adventure movies include the *Hobbit* and *Lord of the Rings* films, and *The Hunger Games.*

- **Comedy:** A film intended to make the audience laugh. Comedies are not easy to write, but they can be great fun to make. Examples of comedy films include *The Lego Movie, Diary of a Wimpy Kid,* and *Night at the Museum.*

- **Crime:** A film involving a crime, usually following the life of a criminal or gangster. Examples of crime films include *The Dark Knight* and the *Fast and Furious* movies.

- **Drama:** A film that focuses on a story and the characters within that story in order to take the audience on an emotional journey. Examples of drama films include *The Theory of Everything, Titanic,* and *Forrest Gump.*

✔ **Fantasy:** A film about magic, myths, legends, and fairy-tales that takes place in a fantasy world. Examples of fantasy films include *Into the Woods, Maleficent,* and the *Harry Potter* films.

✔ **Historical:** A film involving history or that re-creates a historical event. This can include biblical, medieval, or wartime events, among others. Examples of historical films include *Saving Mr. Banks, Lincoln,* and *Amazing Grace.*

✔ **Horror:** A film designed to frighten or shock the audience. Many horror films include monsters, ghosts, vampires, and zombies, often with exaggerated violence and gore. Examples of horror films include *Dracula Untold* and the *Woman in Black* films.

✔ **Musicals:** A film that uses music, songs, and occasionally dance to tell the story. Examples of musicals include *Annie, Grease,* and *Hairspray.*

✔ **Romance:** A film with a story about a love relationship between two characters. Romance films aim to create strong emotions from the audience. Examples of romance films include *The Notebook, Gone with the Wind,* and *The Fault in Our Stars.*

✔ **Science fiction:** A film that involves futuristic technology, aliens, monsters, heroes, space, and things from other worlds. Examples of science fiction films include *Interstellar, Star Wars,* and *Avatar.*

✔ **War:** A film that uses battlefields, fighting, and war to tell the story. Usually these films are based on true events. Examples of war films include *The Imitation Game, War Horse,* and *The Boy in the Striped Pajamas.*

✔ **Westerns:** A film taking place in the American Old West in the late 1800s, usually involving involves horses, gun fighting, cowboys, and Indians. Examples of western films include *The Lone Ranger, Dances with Wolves,* and the *Young Guns* films.

Using a film genre helps the audience understand what to expect from a film. People usually do a bit of research into a film before going to see it, and when a trailer shows that a film is in a genre they find appealing, it may help them make up their minds. For example, people coming home from a long day at work may want a film to cheer them up or make them laugh, so they'd choose to watch a comedy. On the other hand, if they want to watch a film that's a bit more serious or that stirs their emotions, they may choose to watch a drama or a romance.

Most films have more than one genre and fit into more than one category. These include romantic-comedies, action-thrillers, action-comedies, crime-thrillers, and many more.

Have a look through the films on your DVD shelf and see which ones fit into the genres above.

When you have decided on a genre for your film, you need to think about what your story is about. Here are a few things to think about when coming up with an idea:

- **What your audience wants:** It's important to consider your audience: Who are they? What do they want? Don't just come up with ideas that you want to do or that you think will work. Ask your audience — that is, ask people you know who watch your sort of film what they would like to see. Someone may give you the start of an idea that you could develop into a story.

- **There's a story out there:** Many films are based on true stories or events. Perhaps you or someone you know has a story on which you can base your film. Ask around, and see what stories you can find. Most of the films I've written are based on things that have happened to me or people I know. If you can't find a story from people you know, look through a few short story anthologies; the stories there may inspire you.

↙ **What is possible:** Coming up with film ideas about aliens, monsters, and far away planets can be good if you own a spaceship, but you'd do better to consider the sorts of stories you can film with the locations and props you already have around you. For inspiration, have a look around and see what's available to you.

Also, think about who can help you make your trailer: Who will act? Who will help you film? It's also okay to ask people to help you write or come up with ideas. I've written a lot of my films with a writing partner, which is great: One of us may come up with an idea, and the other will throw in more ideas, and the story builds from there.

↙ **No idea is a bad idea:** Write down every idea you have because there is no such thing as a bad idea at this point of the filmmaking process. Any idea you think is bad could easily develop into something great. You may end up writing down loads of ideas you won't use for a while, but it never hurts to have more ideas than you need. Any idea that's useless for your current project could well inspire your next story.

Our film crew will be creating a trailer for a film they'll be shooting later. I'll be using this as a running example in this book. Their film is about a group of children who get lost in a forest and meet a stranger with a mysterious past. The crew haven't fully developed the script for the main film yet, but they have a rough idea of the story and events that happen within the story, which is all they need for the trailer.

After you have come up with an idea for your trailer, the next step is to plan the structure of the trailer and the shots to be filmed.

Structure Your Trailer

Film trailers are created to show the audience what the film is about and to encourage them to want to see it when it's released. It's important to not show too much of the storyline; otherwise people won't want to see the finished film — they'll already know what happens from the trailer! The following list describes a few things you may wish to include in your trailer.

- **A film genre:** When audiences watch a movie trailer, they want to know the genre. By including shots of locations and key moments from your story, your audience can work out the genre of your film. If you were creating a trailer for an action film, you may want to include some of the high energy and action shots from your film. Our crew have chosen a thriller film genre so they have included shots of looking lost and running away, shots of the children hearing noises, and shots of the character they meet.

- **An introduction:** Many trailers include an introduction to the story or character to explain the background or history. Trailers for superhero films usually show clips explaining how they got their superpowers. If you were creating a trailer for a science fiction film, you may want to show clips of your character's life before the aliens invaded. This could be made up of a series of shots building up to the main event in your story. In our crew's film trailer they have included some of the first scene before our characters enter the forest and then a few shots of them playing around in the forest. This helps to introduce the characters and gives some background to the story.

- **Characters:** A trailer is a great opportunity to introduce your audience to the characters in your film. By including important moments from your story and key moments from your actors, your audience can get to know your characters and work out their role in your film. If you were creating a trailer for a crime thriller, you may wish to include moments from the detective characters and any moments from your villains. Include short lines of dialogue to help tell the story and introduce the characters. Our crew have included clips of each character in the story and each character reveals a little bit of the story with what each of them says.

✔ **Emotions:** Audiences like to see emotions and expressions in a trailer as this helps them to understand the emotions they will feel when watching the film. If you were creating a trailer for a horror film, you may want to include clips of your characters looking frightened. In our crew's film trailer, they included clips of the children in the forest looking lost and then getting more and more scared. They included voice clips from the characters, saying things such as "We're not going to make it!" The more shots showing emotions and expressions from your characters you include in your trailer, the more likely you are to engage your audience.

✔ **The ending:** This is an important part of your film trailer because it's where you leave your audience. By the end of the trailer, your audience will make their minds up about your film and whether or not they want to see the full version. You want your audience to turn to the person next to them and say "I really want to see that." To do this, you need to end your trailer with an impact. You could, for instance, aim to leave your audience with a question in mind, wondering what happens next.

Our crew decided to end their trailer with the main character walking away and disappearing as he walks. The aim behind this is to leave the audience wondering who this person is and whether the children made it out of the forest or not.

Have a look through some trailers online to see how other directors do it. It's a good idea to watch a trailer from a film you've already watched to see how its trailer explains the story without giving too much away.

Figure 6-1 shows a structure sheet that our film crew created for their film showing some of the key moments they want to include in their trailer.

You can download a blank version of this structure sheet from this book's companion website.

Film Trailer Structure Sheet

Film Name: __Lost in Time__

Film Genre	Action / Triller

Introduction	- Background to characters - Meet outside forest - One of the group is not sure about going in the forest - They enter the forest - Shots of walking and playing

Characters	Young Luke - Shots of young Luke playing. He wants to stay in forest. He finds the portal Old Luke - Shots of warning the group Hannah - Shots showing wanting to go in forest. She starts to get worried when lost Katie - She is not sure about going in. Tries to get group to go back. Zoe - Wants to go in forest at start but then gets worried, panics.

Emotions	Show different emotions: Confidence about going in Worried about going in Fun / laughter Lost - fear, panic

The Ending	- Shots of running through the forest - Children panic about not getting out - See Old Luke stop them going through time portal - Hear Old Luke's voice as they run - Old luke walking away - disappears

Figure 6-1

List the Shots You Want to Shoot

Before you go out and film your trailer, it's a good idea to list the shots that you want to capture in your trailer first. This helps you keep track of what you have filmed and what you need to film.

Creating a shot list also helps you plan the locations and actors needed for each shot. You may find that you use the same

location more than once but at different points in your film —
such as, say, at the beginning and then at the end of your film.
Instead of filming those two scenes on different days, it would be
easier to film them on the same day. In filmmaking, this is often
done because it saves time and money.

Creating a shot list will be one of the best things you can do to
prepare for filming. Figure 6-2 shows an example of a shot list
from our film crew for their film trailer.

Shot List				
Production Title: Lost in Time Trailer				
Shot No.	Scene No.	Shot Type	Camera Movement	Description
1	1	Wide	Tripod and static	Zoe and Hannah are talking as the rest of the group join them.
2	1	Mid	Tripod with follow	Zoe and Hannah are talking as the rest of the group join them.
3	2	Wide	Tripod with follow	Group walks from behind the camera and into shot. They continue walking away from camera.
4	2	Mid	Handheld	Shot of feet as they walk past camera.
5	2	Wide	Tripod and static	Group walks towards camera looking up at trees.
6	2	Wide	POV and handheld	Point of view from actors looking up at trees.

Figure 6-2

You can download a blank version of this shot list to use on your
own trailer from this book's companion website.

Try It Yourself

Now it's time for you to choose what your trailer is going to be
about. Decide which genres you'll be aiming for and find the idea
on which you will base your story. As you make these decisions,

reflect on other stories that may inspire your trailer, and remember to consider both your audience's expectations and your own limitations, especially your limitations regarding your trailer's budget, setting, and the time you have to devote to it. Make sure your idea ends up being one you can actually achieve.

The next step is to structure your trailer and plan your introduction, think about your characters and the emotions you want to instill in your audience, and then plan your ending. All of these help you choose what you need to film for your trailer.

Finally, list the shots you want to shoot for your trailer using the shot list form. The next step is to shoot and edit your trailer, and I guide you through these processes in the next few projects.

Before you move on to the next project, make sure you're happy with the story for your trailer and that you have included all the shots you want to film in your shot list. Have you explained your story to your family or friends? What do they think? They may have something to add to your trailer. It's important to get the story right before moving on to filming your trailer.

Shooting Your Trailer

It's exciting to get to this point where you can now start to film your trailer. It sometimes feels like it takes ages to get to this point! Even so, it's really important to take the time to prepare for this moment because preparation makes the next steps in making your trailer much easier and quicker.

Your trailer will be made up of short clips from the scenes in your film and sections of dialogue from your characters. It's important to make sure you have selected clips that help to tell your story but that also grab the attention of your audience.

Using your trailer structure sheet or your shot list, you can now gather your crew, actors, and equipment and start filming your trailer. Before you do, however, read carefully over this chapter. Here I show you what you need to do to prepare for filming, and I offer some tips that will help you make your trailer-filming experience better.

Essentials before Shooting

Before you go out and shoot your film, make sure you have everything you need. I've lost count of the number of times I've gone to a location to film and then realized that I forgot something very important, usually batteries, media cards, or cables.

When planning a film, it's good to create a kit list or an equipment list. This is a list of film equipment that you'll need for the film shoot. Each project you work will need a new list because different equipment is needed. Figure 7-1 shows an example of one of my kit lists.

I use this template to tick off the equipment that is needed for each project I work on. When it comes to getting the equipment ready for the shoot, I use this list to make sure I haven't forgotten anything before I make my way to the location.

Directing Your Film

As a director, it's your job to bring the film to life through the way your actors play the characters and how the crew film each shot. The director works with the actors and crew to get the best from them and make sure the story is being told through what they do.

7 Stream Media – Kit List

Project Name: lost in Time Trailer   Date of Filming: 10 / 18 / 14

Cameras
- [ ] Canon C300
- [ ] Canon XF305
- [x] Canon XF105
- [ ] Canon 5D MKii
- [x] Canon 7D

Lenses
- [x] Canon 24-105
- [ ] Samyang 16mm
- [ ] Samyang 35mm
- [ ] Samyang 50mm
- [ ] Samyang 85mm
- [ ] Sigma 50mm

Microphones
- [x] Sony ECM-678
- [ ] Audio Technica
- [ ] Rode NTG2
- [ ] Sennheiser EW100
- [ ] Rode NT2-A

Lights
- [ ] Rotolight Anova x2
- [ ] 500 LED x4
- [ ] 900 LED x2
- [ ] 200 LED x2
- [ ] Rotolight Mini x2
- [x] Mini LEDs x4

Tripods
- [ ] Manfrotto (Silver)
- [x] Vinten
- [ ] Spare

Steadicam
- [ ] Glidecam x 1

Essentials
- (3) [x] Canon Batteries x 7
- (2) [x] CF Cards x 6

Stands
- [ ] Lighting Stands x9
- [ ] Greenscreen system
- [ ] Microphone Stands x3

Greenscreen system
- [ ] Greenscreen 3x3m
- [ ] Greenscreen 4x11m
- [ ] Stands

Monitors/Recorders
- [x] Director monitor

Cables
- [x] Microphone Cables x3
- [ ] Power Cables

Sliders / Dollies
- [ ] Dolly System
- [ ] Slider system

Extras
- [ ] Power Extension x 3
- [ ] Duct Tape
- [ ] Step
- [ ] iPad Stands
- [x] Clapperboard
- [x] Makeup Kit

Figure 7-1

Directing your actors

When filming, the director works closely with the actors to get the best from them and help them perform the character in the way the writer imagined. Because the actors can't see themselves and what they look like while acting, the director can help by offering advice with expressing emotions and delivering lines. This must be done nicely and carefully because you don't want to upset your actors and end up with no one to film. (See Figure 7-2.)

Figure 7-2

Directing your crew

As a director, it's important to know how the camera works and the types of shots that I showed you in Project 2. This helps with explaining to your crew how you want your shots to look. (See Figure 7-3.) The director will normally choose a shot type that helps express the emotion or feeling of the scene. For example, which shot would you use if you wanted to show the fear on the character's face? That's right — you'd use a close-up shot.

What makes a good director?

The following characteristics are important to have as a director:

✔ **Good communication skills:** Directors usually have an idea what the film should look like in their head and they have to try and get that across to the crew and actors. This means they should be good at communicating and explaining what they want.

Figure 7-3

✔ **Confidence:** Directors should be confident in what they want as the crew and actors need to trust that directors know what they are doing. This includes making decisions. If you want to get an extra shot or re-film something, just do it. I have wasted too many hours wondering if I should film something or not and in the time I wasted I could have just re-filmed it.

✔ **Attention to detail:** The director needs to be able to focus on the fine detail of the scene and to be able to do many things at once: watching the actors, what the camera operator is doing, and listening to the dialogue.

The following items are useful for a director to have on-hand during filming:

✔ **Director's monitor:** Often, directors watch a TV monitor that's plugged into the camera so they can see what's happening in the scene. However, don't worry if you don't have one of these monitors. You can direct the scene by looking through the monitor on the camera. Personally, I find it easier to watch the scene through a monitor screen because what the camera sees is normally very different to what you see when you watch a scene directly. It may sound odd but your actor's performance can also look very different through a camera.

- **Script:** Having a script with you is essential as you can check the dialogue from the actors and keep track of where you are in the scene. I like to make notes on my script to remind me of things to capture during scenes and any props or costumes needed for a shot.

- **Storyboard or shot list:** Having a storyboard or a shot list helps the director to keep track of shots filmed and to be filmed. I tend to work mainly from the shot list as I can tick off the shots as they are completed and it helps me to plan the day and see how well we are working to the planned schedule.

When directing your film, it's good to try and picture and imagine the edit in your head as you go. As you film a shot, place it into an imaginary timeline in your head and try and imagine how the shots work together. It may sound odd but it works and it helps me to think of shots I may have missed or think of extra shots and angles that could be filmed to make the scene look even better. It also helps to imagine how the story is coming together, if it's working or not, and if anything needs to change as you film.

You may be worried about how much there is to think about when directing your film, but don't worry, because you will learn as you do it and these things will become natural to you. I've been directing for many years and I'm still learning new things.

Shooting Tips

When shooting your film or trailer, here are a few tips to help enhance your shots.

- **Check for continuity mistakes:** Have you ever watched a film and noticed that the actor has picked something up in his left hand then in the next shot has it in his right hand or there is a glass of coke on the table and it's half full and then in the next shot suddenly it's half empty? This is called a *continuity mistake*. Continuity mistakes often occur in films and involve something in the scene changing between shots, like a prop or actor. On big blockbuster films they normally hire someone to look out for continuity mistakes, but even so, they still happen. If you ask your crew and actors to look out for continuity mistakes, this will reduce the number in your film.

Figure 7-4 shows two shots from the same scene. In the wide shot the actor is holding his bag on his shoulder, but in the mid shot he doesn't have a bag at all. This may have been because both shots were filmed at different times and the actor forgot to pick up his bag for the mid shot. Most of the audience may not notice this error, but there will always be someone who does, so it's best to try and avoid it.

Figure 7-4

Next time you watch a film, look for continuity mistakes where something is different from one shot to the next. Remember, however, to keep these observations to yourself because you don't want to annoy other people watching the film so you end up having to watch films on your own, like me.

✓ **Always get one more take than you need, just to be safe:** You will probably find that you will end up shooting the same shot several times to get the right take, unless you have a perfect cast and crew. A take is one recorded performance in a scene from when the camera operator presses the Record button to when she stops the camera recording. When you do get a good take, you can either carry on to the next shot on your list or get one more take to be safe. I would always get the extra take, because your actors might deliver an even better performance or there might have been a mistake or problem in the last take that you didn't notice. You might not be popular with the actors or crew for doing this, but it's always better to have more takes to choose from when editing.

✔ **Shoot out of order:** Most films are shot out of sequence, which means that the scenes are shot in a different order to how they appear in the film. The reason for this is to make the filming process as simple and easy as possible. For example, you may have two or more scenes that are filmed in the same location but appear at different times in the final edited film. Instead of filming one scene at that location and then coming back on another day to the same location to film another scene, you could just film both scenes on the same day in the same location. It may mean that your actors have to change their clothes to make it look like it's a different day, but that is much easier than having to go back to that location and set up and film again. This also applies to locations in a house. You may have two or more scenes in the kitchen that appear at different times in the film. Again, you can film both scenes in the kitchen one after the next to save time having to move to another location and then come back to the kitchen and have to set up and film again. This is often done on big blockbuster films because it saves money as hiring locations can be expensive.

Checking Your Shots

Checking your footage after each scene you film should become a habit. Sometimes I like to check shots straight after they have been filmed before I move on to the next shot. The last thing you want to do is import your footage at the end of the day and find there are problems with your footage and you can't use it in the edit. Trust me, I've been there.

When I first started making films, I once filmed a whole day of footage and didn't check the shots after every scene. When I got around to importing the footage onto my computer, I found that there was an issue with the camera and the footage was no good. I couldn't use any of the shots that I filmed that day. I then had to rearrange the shoot for another day, call the actors and crew back in, and buy them all lunch to say sorry. I will never do that again and I always check the shots at least after every scene.

The reasons to check your footage include:

- ✔ **Technical issues:** You may an issue with your camera or have dirt on your lens that you may not notice during filming. This is something you will notice when you play it back on a larger monitor or by importing it onto your computer.

- ✔ **Continuity and mistakes:** You may find that you miss or don't see mistakes while filming. This could be an actor stumbling over a word or something in a shot that shouldn't be. I once filmed a scene with a light in a shot and only noticed when we checked the shots.

- ✔ **Missed shots:** When you look back through your footage, it's a great opportunity to double-check that you have filmed all the shots on your shot list or storyboard and not missed any. Missing shots is very easy to do and can cause problems when editing.

By checking your footage after each scene you can always reshoot any missed shots, or if needed, reshoot the scene without having to book your location, actors, and crew again and come back on another day.

If your camera records using tapes instead of media cards, then the process of checking your footage is a little more complicated.

After watching the footage back from the tape you should make sure you play to the end of the last take you shot so that your camera doesn't record over any of the scenes you already shot. The safest way to do this is to record a placeholder at the end of every scene, before you rewind the tape to check the footage. A placeholder is just a few seconds of blank video, perhaps shot with the lens cap on, or, if your camera has them, you could use color bars to record the placeholder. If you go the lens-cap route, however, always be sure you take the cap back off for the next shot!

Try It Out Yourself

In the first few projects of this book, I show you how the camera works, how to record and import footage, how to frame different types of shots, how to record sound, and how to light your scenes. With this information and the skills you've developed in this project, you can now call in your actors and crew and go out and film your trailer. Don't worry about making mistakes; the more you practice your new skills, the more you will grow as a filmmaker. You can always revisit some of the first few chapters to refresh your memory.

Remember to make a list of equipment you need, look out for continuity mistakes, and check the shots before moving on to the next scene. In the next project, you edit the footage for your film trailer together.

Setting the Pace and Mood with Editing

It's now time to see what your trailer footage looks like. In this project, you bring your film footage to life and set the mood and pace of your film trailer.

When editing, "setting the pace and mood" means to create the feel and emotion of your film. This can be done by the way the shots look, the type of shots you use, the length of time you stay on a shot in the timeline, or the mood of the music you use. It's important that the feel and look of your trailer matches the genre of your film. If your film is a romance, for example, you don't want to change the shots too often, and you may want to include shots that clearly tell the audience it's a romance, such as when two characters look lovingly into each other's eyes, or find music that fits the mood. Scary or creepy music, of course, is not going to work for a romance.

Our film crew created a thriller film trailer about a group of young people who find themselves lost in a forest. To get the feel of a thriller across when editing, we have to capture the expressions and emotions from the actors and add music that matches these emotions.

Our crew decided to keep the length of their shots short, and to include shots that show fear from the characters and use music that has a creepy and scary feel.

In this project, I show you how to make your trailer look great and how to match it to the genre you've chosen.

Arranging Your Footage on the Timeline

In Project 5, I showed you how create an event and a project, how to import your footage, and how to place selected clips onto the timeline. Now, in this project I show you how to arrange the footage on the timeline to create your trailer.

Before I start editing I always make sure that I have a copy of the script or shot list in front of me to work from. This helps me know the order in which to place the clips and ensure I don't miss any clips.

You can start arranging your trailer footage on your timeline by following these steps.

1. **Import your trailer footage into your new event in iMovie and create a new project with your film name followed by the word *Trailer*.**

2. **Select the clip that you'd like to appear first in your trailer and drag it to the start of your timeline, as shown in Figure 8-1.**

3. **Add the next clip to the timeline after the first clip.**

   At the moment, don't worry about trimming the clips. You might want to do that when you add the music later. You should now have your first two clips in your timeline, as shown in Figure 8-2.

Figure 8-1

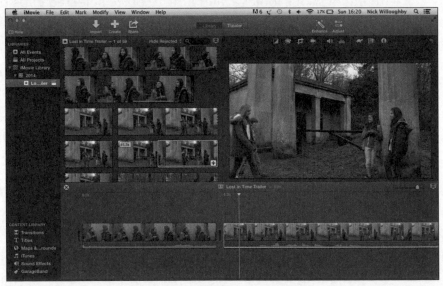

Figure 8-2

4. **Continue to add the clips to your timeline in the order on your shot list.**

5. **If you need to swap a clip with another, click and hold on the clip you want to move and drag it to the position you want it to be and let go, as shown in Figure 8-3.**

Figure 8-3

Adding Music

Adding music really enhances your trailer. Make sure you select music that suits the genre of your film. If you intend to distribute your film, or to post it for public view, be sure to check whether the music you use is legally available and that you have permission to use it. Permissions can be very complicated, but our team used music from www.incompetech.com, which has songs created by Kevin MacLeod. At the moment, Kevin doesn't charge for his music as long as you add his name to your film credits. If you don't want to add music credits at the end of your film, you can pay Kevin for a license to use his music.

Royalty-free music is the kind you pay for only once, giving you a license to use the music on your film without having to pay again every time the film is played or purchased. Besides incompetech. com, other royalty-free music sites include www.revostock.com and www.premiumbeat.com, each of which offers a variety of affordable music tracks to buy and download. Another site is www.smartsound.com, which also offers affordable music tracks but additionally offers Sonicfire, which is software that can be used to match the length of a music file to the length of your video in your timeline.

Our film crew chose to use Kevin MacLeod's track "Interloper." After you have downloaded the track you'd like to use, follow these steps to add it to your timeline:

1. **Click the Import button in the top toolbar.**

2. **Using the drives shown in the pane on the left-hand side, navigate to the music track you wish to use.**

3. **Select the music track and click Import Selected, as shown in Figure 8-4.**

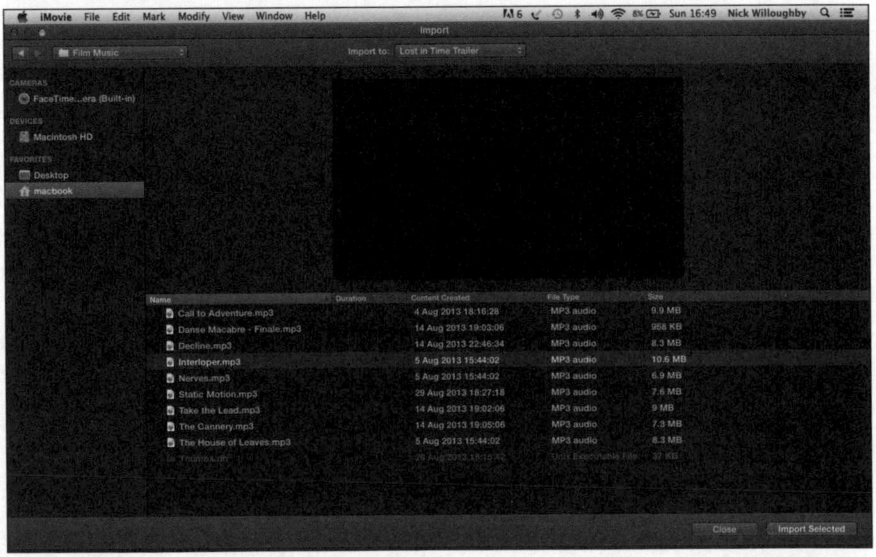

Figure 8-4

Your music track now appears with your clips in the event, as shown in Figure 8-5. All audio tracks are shown as green clips with audio waveforms within.

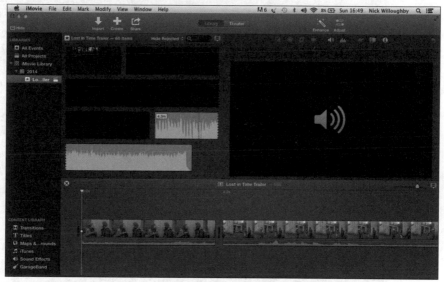

Figure 8-5

You can listen to the music track by hovering over the music clip and pressing the spacebar on your keyboard.

4. **To bring your music track under your video clips in the timeline, first click and drag over the music track in the event window to select the part of the music track you want to use, as shown in Figure 8-6.**

5. **Click and drag the selected area of the music track under the video at the beginning of your timeline, as shown in Figure 8-7.**

In Figure 8-7, the waveform of the music appears in the clip. The waveform looks like a mountain range, showing the loud and quiet areas of the music. As you can see in the track, there is a quiet section at the beginning that I could get rid of.

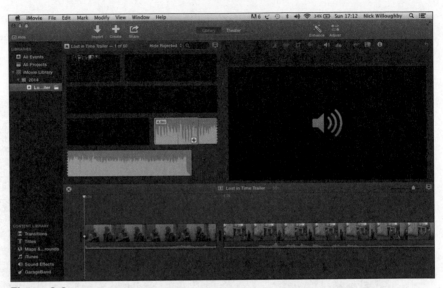

Figure 8-6

Figure 8-7

6. You can adjust the length of the music track by selecting the music track in the timeline and clicking and holding at the front of the track and dragging to the left or right, and then release the mouse button when you are done trimming (See Figure 8-8).

Figure 8-8

7. **Drag the whole clip over to the start so the music starts as my first clip does, as shown in Figure 8-9.**

Figure 8-9

You may also want to adjust the length of the music because your trailer should be about 60 seconds long. Your music track is likely to be longer than that, so you must trim it down to be about one minute in length.

8. **Some of your video clips may have sound that you don't want. To remove the sound from a video clip, hover over the line between the video and audio within the clip, as shown in Figure 8-10.**

Your cursor should turn into two arrows pointing up and down.

Figure 8-10

9. **Click, hold, and drag the line down to the bottom of the clip, as shown in Figure 8-11.**

10. **To make the music fade out at the end of your track, scroll to the end of the music track and select the track.**

When it's selected, a small circle appears midway up at the end of the track. Click and hold on this circle and drag to the left.

Figure 8-11

This creates a fade at the end of the music track, as shown in Figure 8-12.

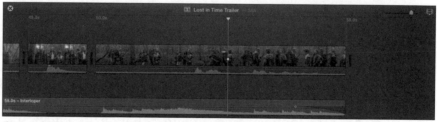

Figure 8-12

Now we can adjust the video clips to match the music. Because this is a trailer, try to keep your clips short to give a taste of what is in your film.

11. **To adjust the length of a clip, select the clip and hover your mouse pointer at the end or start of the clip.**

When you do so, two arrows appear, pointing left and right. Click, hold, and drag the end or start of the clip left or right to make it shorter or longer, as shown in Figure 8-13.

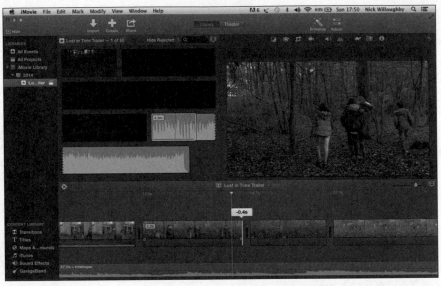

Figure 8-13

You may wish to add some transitions to your trailer, but remember, you don't want too many transitions. If you need help with adding transitions, revisit Project 5.

Adjusting Brightness and Contrast

One of the ways you can change the look of your video is to adjust the brightness and contrast. *Brightness* simply changes how light or dark the footage looks. *Contrast* changes the light areas and shadows of the footage at the same time. Increasing the contrast lightens the light areas and darkens the shadows in your shot, making the footage look more rich and vibrant. Decreasing the contrast, on the other hand, darkens the light areas and lightens the shadows, making your footage look more cloudy and dull.

After you have adjusted your clips to the music and added the transitions, now you can adjust the brightness and contrast of your clips by following these steps:

1. **Select the first clip on your timeline and click Adjust in the top toolbar above the preview monitor, as shown in Figure 8-14.**

Figure 8-14

This reveals tools to adjust and change the look of the selected video clip.

2. **To adjust the contrast or brightness of your image, click the Color Correction button, as shown in Figure 8-15.**

This brings up options to adjust the brightness and contrast, the saturation, and the color temperature. For now, adjust the brightness and contrast. Saturation and color temperature are explained in more detail in Project 21.

3. **To make the whole video brighter or darker, move the slider button marked B in Figure 8-16 left or right.**

When our crew filmed their trailer, it was starting to get dark. They decided to carry on, knowing that we could adjust the image later, when editing. Some of the shots towards the end

Figure 8-15

of the shoot are a bit dark so these will need brightening up using this method.

4. **To make the bright areas of your video clip lighter or darker, move the slider button marked C in Figure 8-16 left or right.**

   To improve the look of the video clips, I prefer to make the lighter areas of the video a bit lighter. If the clip is over-exposed then I would darken the lighter areas using this method.

5. **To make the dark areas of your video clip lighter or darker, move the slider button marked A in Figure 8-16 left or right.**

   To give a more filmlike look, I like to make the darker areas a little bit darker but not too much as you can lose the detail in the shadowed areas.

I show you how to use some of the other color correction functions and effects in Project 21.

Figure 8-16

Adding Titles

Titles are words that appear over the footage in a film or video and are used to tell the audience information. Most titles appear at the beginning of a film to tell the audience the name of the film and maybe information about the filmmakers. Sometimes titles are used in films to give information about a scene, date, or location — such as "Two years later," or "London, England" — that's essential for the audience to know.

You may want to add a title at the beginning of your trailer with the title of your film. Titles can be added over video or over blank video before the video clips. Titles can also be added at any point in your timeline. For now, however, start by adding a title at the beginning of your trailer by following these steps:

1. **Click on the Titles button in the content library, as shown in Figure 8-17.**

   This brings up a list of titles to choose from.

Figure 8-17

2. **To see what the titles look like, click on the start of the title and press the spacebar, as shown in Figure 8-18.**

Figure 8-18

3. When you have found the title you want to use, click, hold, and drag the title onto the start of your timeline, as shown in Figure 8-19.

   We chose the title called "Focus" because it fit the genre of the film.

Figure 8-19

4. When you have dragged the title into the timeline, the preview monitor will show your title with the text highlighted. Enter your title, as shown in Figure 8-20.

5. If you want to change the font type, select the text in your title box and click open the Font drop-down box above the preview monitor. Select a font from the list of fonts available, as shown in Figure 8-21.

6. If you want to change the font size, select the text in your title box and click the Text Size drop-down box above the preview monitor. Select a size from those available or enter in your own number, as shown in Figure 8-22.

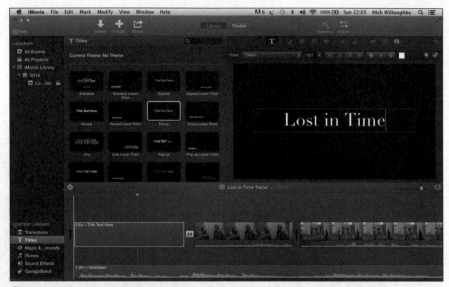

Figure 8-20

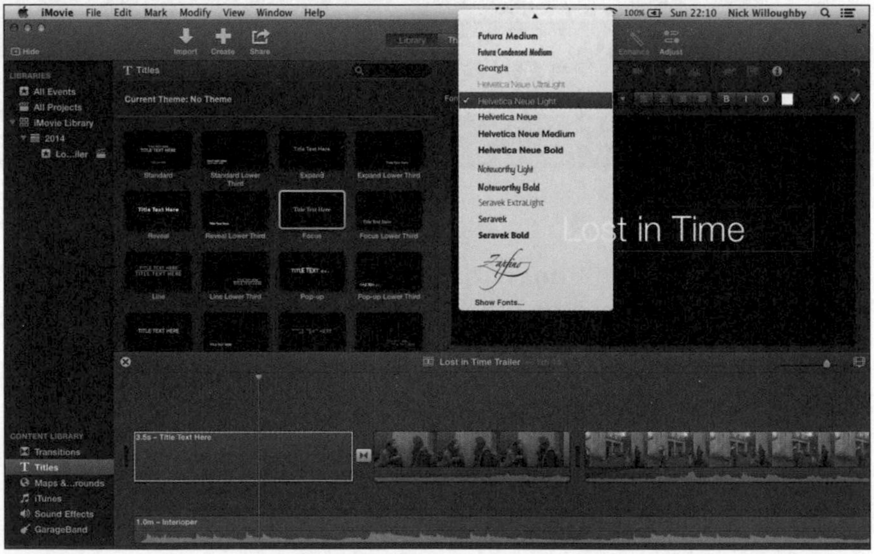

Figure 8-21

7. You can now watch your title and trailer by clicking at the start of your timeline and pressing the spacebar.

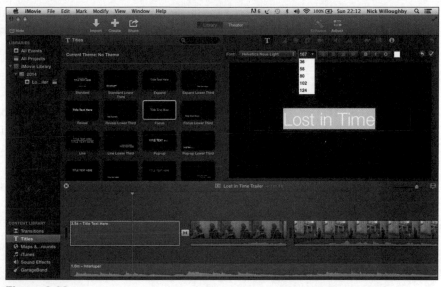

Figure 8-22

You may want to add a dissolve transition between the title and the first clip in your timeline so that the title fades into the first clip.

If you used music from Kevin MacLeod and didn't pay for a license, remember to add a title at the end of the video (such as "Music by Kevin MacLeod") to credit him for the music.

After you've completed editing your trailer, you can now export your video to share with your family and friends.

Sharing Your Film on YouTube

Sharing your film with your family and friends is great, but you may want to reach a wider audience. Sharing the film on a video-hosting site like YouTube is a way to do that. The library of videos on YouTube gets billions of views every day, and some videos there have been viewed hundreds of millions of times.

Uploading your film to YouTube allows you to share a link to your film with friends and family around the world and get comments and reviews. Before uploading your films to YouTube, however, make sure you have permission from a parent to do so.

Sharing your film to YouTube from iMovie

To upload your film to YouTube through iMovie, follow these steps:

1. **Make sure you have a YouTube account to which you can upload your film.**

You must be at least 13 years old to have a YouTube account so you may want to ask your parent's permission to use his or her account or ask him or her to set an account up.

2. **Open your trailer within iMovie.**

3. **Click Share in the top toolbar, as shown in Figure 8-23.**

   This shows a list of sharing options for your film.

Figure 8-23

4. **Click the YouTube logo, as shown in Figure 8-24.**

   This shows the setting options for your video before it's
   uploaded to YouTube. Here you can choose to change the title,
   description of the video, and category, and you can define who
   can see the video when it's shared.

Figure 8-24

5. **Click in the title box to change the title, if necessary, and
   add a description about the film by clicking in the description box, as shown in Figure 8-25.**

Figure 8-25

6. You can then add *tag words,* which are words or phrases that are related to your film, and which allow people to be able to search for it. The tag words we used appear in Figure 8-25.

7. You can also select the size of your video here. However, I recommend leaving this at the default setting.

8. Then set the category. (Use "Film & Animation" unless there's a good reason to do otherwise.) Then, change the privacy settings to "Public," as shown in Figure 8-26.

   You can leave the privacy settings at "Private," if you want to prevent people you don't know from viewing your film.

9. Click the Sign In button in the bottom-left corner of the window, as shown in Figure 8-26.

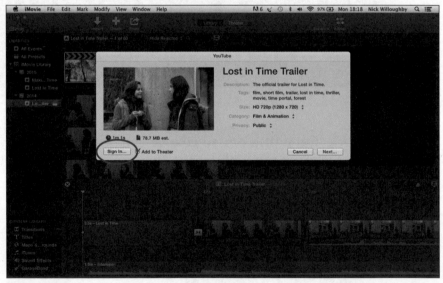

Figure 8-26

10. Sign into your account using the form shown in Figure 8-27. Then click OK.

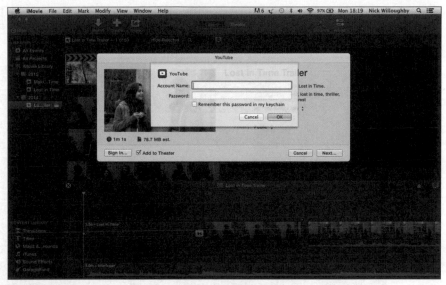

Figure 8-27

11. Click Next, as shown in Figure 8-28.

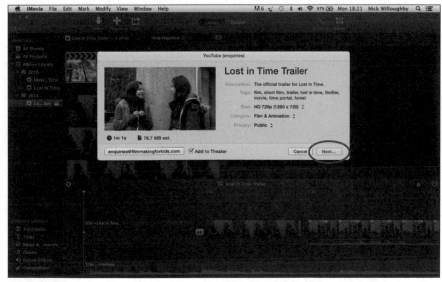

Figure 8-28

12. **Read the "YouTube Terms of Service." If you agree to these terms, click the Publish button, as shown in Figure 8-29.**

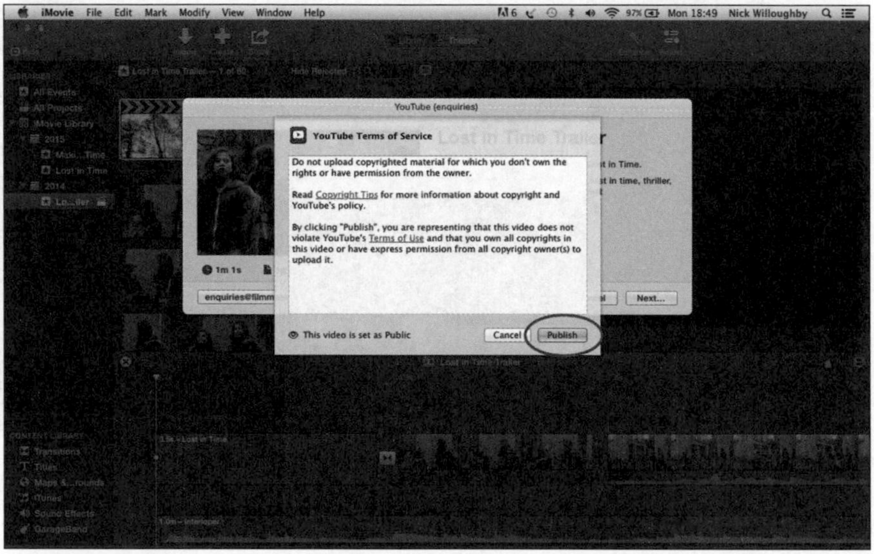

Figure 8-29

Your film is now uploaded to your account on YouTube. When it's been uploaded, you'll see a notification in the top-right corner of the screen confirming this, as shown in Figure 8-30.

Upload your film through YouTube

If you didn't use iMovie to edit your film and want to upload your film onto YouTube through the YouTube site, follow these steps:

1. **Open the YouTube website and log in to your YouTube account.**

2. **Click Upload in the top-right corner of the web page, as shown in Figure 8-31.**

3. **Click Select Files to Upload, as shown in Figure 8-32.**

Notification

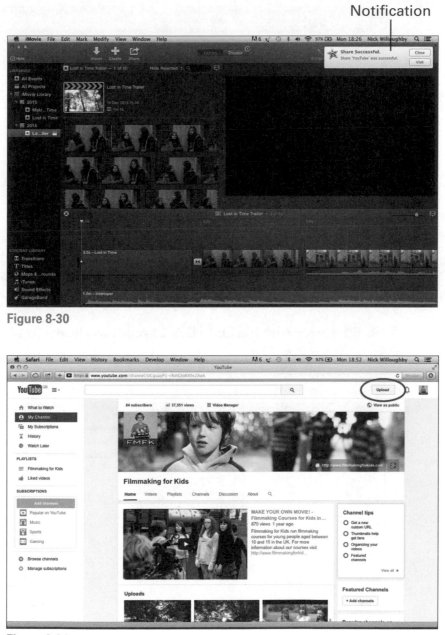

Figure 8-30

Figure 8-31

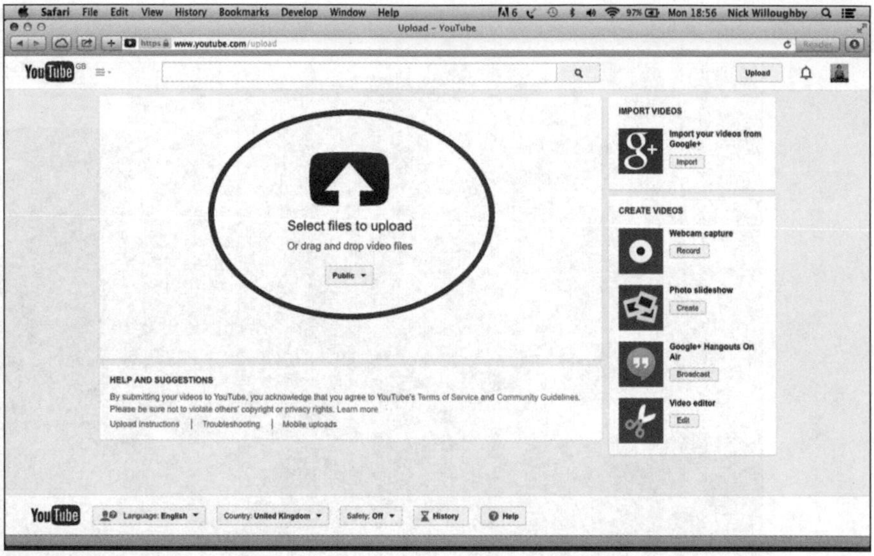

Figure 8-32

4. **Find your film file and click Choose, as shown in Figure 8-33.**

Your film now starts uploading.

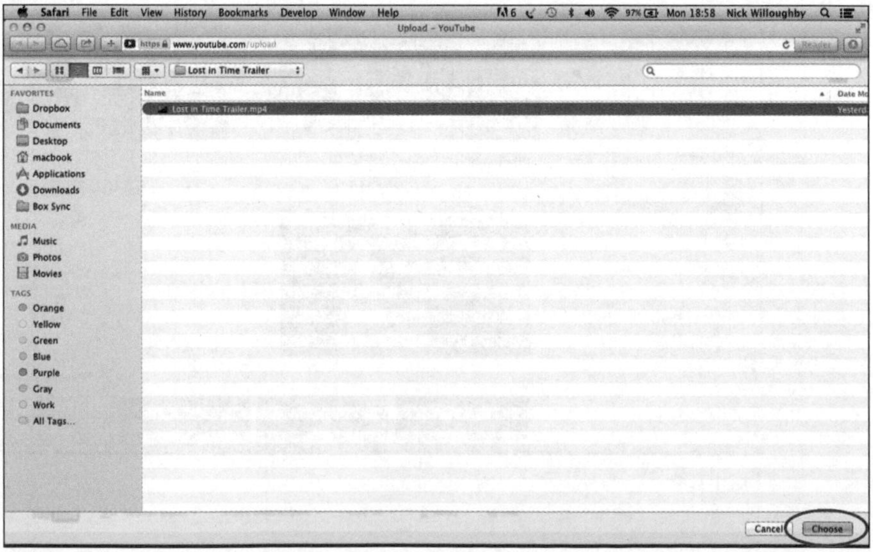

Figure 8-33

A progress bar shows the upload process, as shown in Figure 8-34.

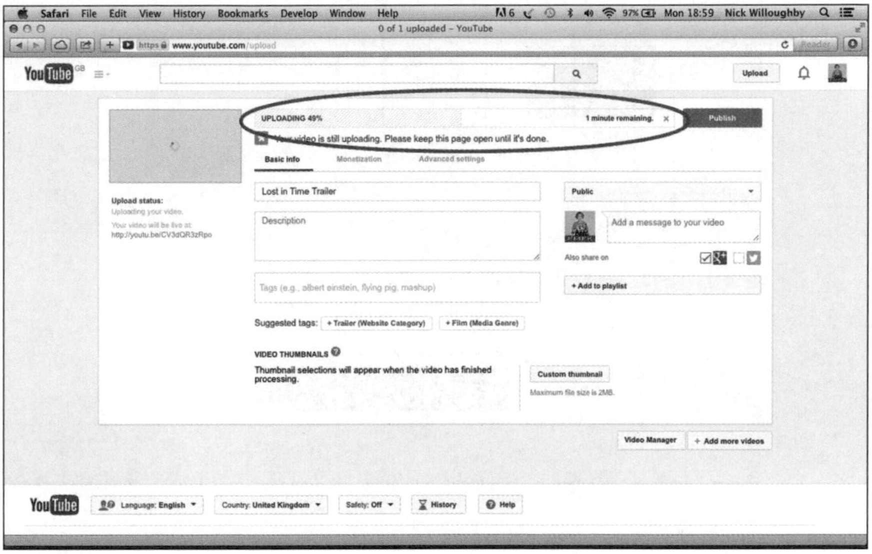

Figure 8-34

5. **Enter your film's title and description, as shown in Figure 8-35.**

6. **You can then add *tag words*, which are words or phrases that are related to your film, and which allow people to be able to search for it.**

The tag words we used appear in Figure 8-35.

7. **Choose a video thumbnail for your film from the three suggested thumbnails below the tags box, as shown in Figure 8-36.**

Thumbnails are still images that are used as the preview image for the video on your channel or in the search results. Try to choose a thumbnail that represents your film the best.

8. **Click open the Advanced Settings tab, as shown in Figure 8-37.**

Title   Description

Figure 8-35

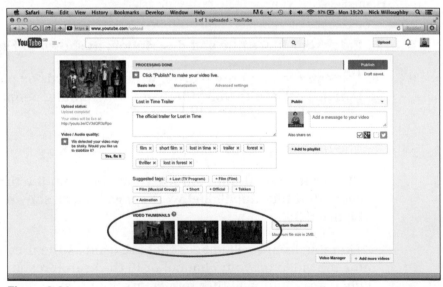

Figure 8-36

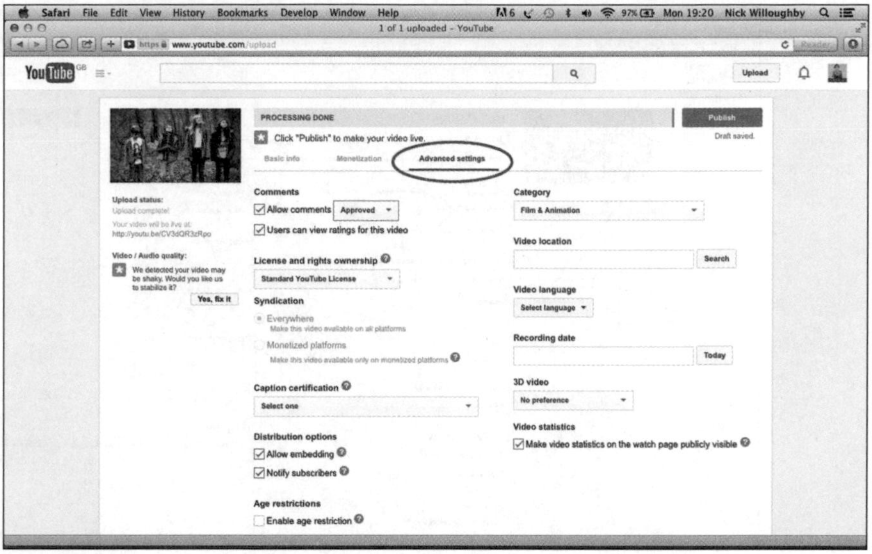

Figure 8-37

Here you can choose to accept comments on your video or not. I always set my comments settings to "Approved," which means I can review and approve any comments before they are posted to my video.

9. **To approve comments before they are posted to your video, click the Allow Comments drop-down box and select "Approved," as shown in Figure 8-38.**

10. **To complete and release your video on YouTube, click Publish in the top-right corner of the web page, as shown in Figure 8-39.**

Your video is now on YouTube. When it's published, YouTube will send you an email with the link to your video. You can now share this link with your family and friends.

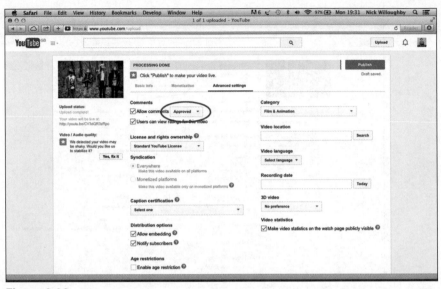

Figure 8-38

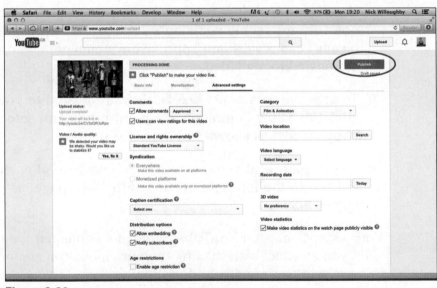

Figure 8-39

Week 3
Making a
Documentary

This week you'll . . .

To view the documentary our young crew made, see www.dummies.com/extras/digitalfilmmakingforkids. Here you can also find a video with tips on interviewing your subjects.

What Makes a Good Documentary?

A documentary or info-film is a great way to present any topic you're interested in to an audience using the art of filmmaking. What makes a documentary good is simply the story and the way it's presented.

Making a documentary is very different to making a story-based fictional film because it's usually more about the research, the story, and the information presented than the creative look and feel of the film.

A good documentary maker should be impartial, which means she should not reveal her own opinions or feelings on the topic of the film in the film itself. Opinions on the subject of the film should be contributed only by the characters and subjects appearing in the film. A good documentary presents both sides of a story and avoids hiding any information or facts from the audience. It simply presents the information in an interesting and creative way.

What Is a Documentary?

A *documentary* is a non-fiction genre of film that documents or captures a real story. It's a way of presenting factual information about real-life events and stories to an audience using real people. Documentary makers usually film hours and hours of footage and then choose the best moments to include in the final edit as the aim is to captivate the audience to keep them watching.

An example of a good documentary is *March of the Penguins* (2005), which follows the journey of Emperor penguins as they migrate to their breeding ground. It has some amazing footage of penguins and a great voiceover by Morgan Freeman. Another example of a good documentary is *Blackfish* (2008), which is about the dangers of keeping killer whales in captivity.

Documentaries shown on TV are normally between 30 minutes and an hour long, but the documentary you will be making in this part of the book will probably be closer to about 5 minutes in length.

Documentary Film Styles

There are different styles and ways to present information in a documentary. The style you choose should depend on the way you think the information should be presented and the style you think would best suit the audience you're aiming at. The following list explains more about the different styles you can use within your documentary film:

- **Direct:** A traditional way of presenting information usually using a voiceover to explain to the audience directly what's being shown onscreen. Wildlife documentaries are normally shot this way. This style is not the most creative way of shooting a documentary, but it's a simple and effective way of presenting information to an audience.

- **Fly-on-the-wall:** This style of documentary filmmaking is mainly used to present events or real-life situations in which the camera follows someone around. In this style, most of the story is told through the subjects. Fly-on-the-wall filmmakers often use smaller cameras with onboard sound so they can blend more easily into a situation without causing too much of a distraction. Because this style doesn't normally include a voiceover to guide the audience through the story, audience members are left to make up their own minds about the topic or situation being filmed.

✔ **Interactive:** This style uses interviews from the subjects involved in the story. Subjects are asked questions about the story, and their answers are used to tell the story in the film. Usually the interview questions are cut out to make it seem as though the subject is telling the story directly to the audience. The interactive style is often used within other styles of documentary making.

✔ **Presented:** In this style of documentary filmmaking, the filmmaker (or another person) presents the story to the camera. The presenter becomes part of the film and guides the audience through the story and interviews people along the way. Often the presenter's feelings and emotions about the topic are shown through this method of documentary filmmaking.

You don't have to stick within one style, of course. You can blend or mix different styles within your film, which can be more engaging for your audience. Our crew is making a documentary about the making of their short film, *Lost in Time*. They have decided to use a mixture of styles, including using the direct style with a voiceover to introduce the topic and explain about the film, the fly-on-the-wall style to show behind-the-scenes shots, and the interactive style to show interviews from the cast and crew involved in making their film.

In this chapter, I show you how to choose a topic and to structure your documentary film so that it's ready for shooting.

Picking a Topic for Your Documentary

It's a good idea to choose a topic that interests you, because it's your interest that will drive you to complete the film. It's also important to choose a topic that you think your audience will enjoy or find interesting. No matter how enthusiastic you are, making a documentary about paint drying really won't captivate any audience.

You may wish to make a documentary about your hobby or a friend's hobby, about an event you're attending, about your school, or about a charity you support. Whatever you choose, make sure it's possible to film and that you have people you can interview about the topic. Our film crew chose to make their documentary about the making of a short film they've been writing and filming. Their documentary film will show behind-the-scenes footage and include interviews from the cast and crew.

It's important to be clear about the aim and purpose of your film. What do you want to tell your audience? Is it to promote an event or group? Is it to present information? Is it to reveal a truth or to prove a point? Think about what your audience will take away from your documentary film and how they will feel. If you're making a film about your hobby, do you want to encourage others to take part? If you're making a film about a charity, do you want your audience to donate or help? All these questions can help you know how you want to present your film.

Researching your topic is one of the most important tasks when creating your documentary. The more research you do, the more confident you can be with the information you're presenting. You could potentially end up giving incorrect information to your audience. It's always a good idea to check through your facts and information several times before filming, and to get others to check through to make sure you haven't missed anything. Imagine promoting a party or event and getting the date or time wrong. You could end up with a lot of unhappy partiers turning up on the wrong day.

Structuring Your Documentary Film

Planning your documentary film is essential because you want to make sure you have all the information needed before you start filming. When you've done your research and you have all the information about your topic you need, you can structure your info film in a way that captures the attention and interest of your audience.

Like any good story, your documentary needs a strong beginning, middle, and end to keep your audience interested and watching. Breaking your documentary into three sections helps to structure the information you want to include, as follows:

- **Introduction:** Your introduction should captivate your audience and make them want to watch more. Here is a great opportunity to tell your audience what your documentary film is about and what you will be including in the main section. Most documentaries have a short introduction at the start to introduce the topic, the characters, and subjects. The documentary our crew is making will include a short introduction with a voiceover to introduce the audience to the making of the film. The introduction will also include clips from interviews from the main section to introduce the cast and crew from the film. This gives the audience a little taste of what is to come and what to expect.

- **The body or main section:** This is where you tell your story with your interviews, voiceovers, and video clips. It's an opportunity to explore your topic and to pick out the interesting information or the moments you would like to present to your audience. It's also a chance to get to know the characters and understand why they're involved in your info film. In our crew's documentary, the main section will include interviews from the cast and crew of the film, video clips to go with the interviews, and facts and information about how the film was made and what inspired the story. The aim here is to present information that the audience may not know and to promote the film.

- **Conclusion:** Ending your film with a conclusion can help the audience members make up their minds about the information you've presented. Your conclusion summarizes the main points covered in your film and brings the story to a natural end, leaving your audience feeling informed. This may include the answer to a question asked in the introduction, or the end of a journey started in the introduction. You may wish to include information about the subject at the end of your info film with a *call to action,* which is a way the audience can respond to what they have just watched. Calls to action are often used with charity or promotional films that leave information (such as a website or telephone number) at the end. The conclusion for our crew's documentary includes some final quotes from the film crew and cast about how they felt about making the film and what they enjoyed most.

Your job as a documentary filmmaker is to present information to your audience without showing your feelings or opinions on the topic. The audience should be allowed to decide what to think and how to feel about the information you have presented to them.

Make a list

When I make a documentary, I make a list of all the information and items I want to include in the film and then create a list of my character interviews. I then put this list into an order that I think will keep my audience interested throughout the film. I find it useful to think of my audience throughout the whole process. Imagining the way the audience feels and the questions they may ask helps me choose the information to include in the film. With my list of information and items complete, I then create a shot list, which shows every shot to include in the film. Figure 9-1 shows part of the shot list our crew created for their info film.

Tell your story

At this point, you should think about how you're going to tell your story. Documentaries can be told in different ways, such as through the use of a voiceover or through what your characters and subjects say. A voiceover is a popular way to narrate such films, but I prefer to let my characters tell the story because this can feel more natural. Our crew decided to introduce their film with a voiceover and then use the subjects to tell the story through interviews.

If you are using a voiceover, write the script before filming. This helps to create a shot list and to structure your film. Your voiceover

Shot List

Project Title: Making of Lost in Time – Info Film

Shot No.	Scene No.	Shot Type	Camera Movement	Description
1	1	Wide	Tripod	Shot of group filming first scene
2	1	Mid	Handheld	Shot of group filming first scene
3	1	Close	Handheld	Over-the-shoulder shot of camera operator
4	2	Mid	Handheld	Film crew walking through forest
5	2	Close	Handheld	Spot interview with Nick
6	2	Wide	Handheld	Shot from behind crew – Scene 2

Figure 9-1

should always present information; it should never have an opinion. On the other hand, if you're using your characters to tell your story, be sure to have a list of questions to ask them.

Write interview questions

In Project 10, I share some techniques for filming interviews, but before you get to that, take a look at this list of things to think about when writing the questions to ask in those interviews. Asking open-ended questions can help you avoid one-word answers. You may also want to ask two questions together to get the most out of the answer.

✔ **Who?** Whom will you interview? Your interviews can play an important part in your film, so choose your subjects and characters carefully. Choose people who are confident enough to talk on camera and have the knowledge to answer the questions clearly. You may wish to include information about your subjects and characters in your documentary, so think about the questions you could ask to get this information. Our team included questions like, "What is your role in the film?" and "How did you get involved in the film?"

✔ **What?** Think about what you'll ask your subjects or characters to get more information about the topic. You may wish to ask questions about their experiences and how they are involved in the topic to show their knowledge. Our crew asked questions like, "What can you tell me about your experience with the film?" and "What inspired the story?"

✔ **When?** If you're creating a documentary film about an event or a party, then the date and time are quite important. You may want to ask your subjects or characters questions about when they do something or how often they do it. Our crew asked their characters questions like, "How long have you been interested in filmmaking?" and "How long did it take to create this film?"

✔ **Where?** You may wish to include questions about the location or venue of the topic, if it's needed. You could film your interview in a place that's connected with the topic. Our crew filmed some of the interviews on-location during the filming and asked questions like, "Tell me about where you're filming today?" and "What has happened in the filming so far?"

✔ **Why?** Using *why* in your questions is a great way to get more information out of a character or subject during the interview. Questions beginning with *why* are simple, but they're more likely to give you longer and more emotional answers. Our crew asked questions like, "Why did you get involved with this film?" and "What have you enjoyed the most?"

Try It Out Yourself

So, now it's time to choose a topic for your documentary film. After you've chosen a topic, think about how you're going to present your information and the style you'll use to do it. Create a structure for your film and make sure you've researched the topic thoroughly. Create a shot list for your info film.

In the next project, I show you how to film the interviews and other footage that will appear in your documentary film.

Shooting Your Documentary

It's now time to shoot your documentary using your shot list and your list of questions to ask your characters and subjects. Take the time to prepare and make sure you have filmed everything you need. It'll make editing your film a lot easier.

Remember, a documentary is a fact-based, non-fiction film, so it's important to present the information in your documentary as accurately and truthfully as possible and to respect the subjects you are working with. Also, remember that it's important to avoid showing your opinions or feelings throughout your documentary.

In this chapter, I show you how to shoot a documentary that you will be proud to show your friends and family.

Create a Short Summary to Introduce Your Topic

The summary at the beginning of your documentary is a great way to introduce the topic. This summary can be made up of footage and interview clips from the main section. You could also write a voiceover to help introduce the topic. I often create the introduction summary toward the end of filming, because I know what I can use from the footage I have already filmed.

Expect your introduction summary to be about 30 seconds long — long enough to introduce the topic, inform your audience, and capture their interest. Think of the introduction summary is a trailer for the main section. The following list describes the sort of clips you might use to add to your introduction summary:

✔ Clips that explain what the topic is about

✔ Clips that introduce your characters

✔ Video footage from the main section to support the information in the introduction

✔ Any interesting moments captured in the main section

✔ Any history or background information about your topic or characters

✔ Clips that explain the aim or reason for your documentary

To help create your introduction summary, you may find it useful to watch other documentaries. You may even be able to find existing documentaries on the topic you have chosen. Our crew watched many behind-the-scenes documentaries before creating a structure and a list of interview questions for their own documentary. There is nothing wrong with learning from other filmmakers by watching how they do it.

Interviewing Techniques

If your documentary will include interviews, you may wish to shoot them first, because your subjects' answers may help you choose what to include in the rest of the documentary.

The subjects that you are interviewing are unlikely to be actors or people used to being on camera, so it's very likely that they'll be nervous, and they may make mistakes. It's your job as a filmmaker and director to make them feel as comfortable as possible. You can do this by introducing yourself and your role within the film and by explaining to them what will happen during filming and what you would like them to do.

Many interview subjects think that they only have one chance to get their answers right, which may make them feel more nervous. Try to keep them calm. Explain that you're there to help them, and that they can retake the interview if necessary. Allow the subjects to practice their answers in front of the camera: This may help them feel more comfortable and allow them to think about what they're going to say.

Framing your subject

When shooting your interviews, remember to use the framing techniques discussed in Project 2 and the lighting techniques discussed in Project 4.

If you have extra lights you can use, consider using the three-point lighting technique for the interviews. Make sure you set up the lighting and equipment before your subject arrives. You want to be sure both you and your subject are as comfortable as possible. If you're still setting up when the subject arrives, you'll be under pressure to get started quickly. This is how mistakes often happen.

It's also important to think in advance about how you'll record sound. Do you have an external microphone you can use or will you be using the onboard microphone? Remember to check for background noises and any other distractions while filming the interviews.

Mid shots and close-up shots give the most natural look to an interview. Sometimes I use both. I start with a mid shot for the first question, change to a close-up for the second question, and then back to a mid shot for the third. This means I can cut out the questions from the interviewer when editing, leaving just the answers. When these pieces are assembled together, this can look like one long answer from the subject and that I changed the camera angle as he or she moved from one answer to the next.

Make sure the interviewer stays quiet while the subject is answering the questions because you don't want any interruptions from off-camera noises or laughter. Removing background noises during editing can be difficult and sometimes impossible.

Figure 10-1 shows how our team framed the mid shot and close-up shot in their interviews. Remember to use the rule of thirds. (See Project 2.)

Figure 10-1

Looking off-camera

Many filmmakers film interviews with the subject looking away from the camera because this can be more comfortable for the audience to watch. Figure 10-1 shows you how this looks. Your subjects should look at the camera only when they're talking directly to the audience. This technique is mainly used when filming TV presenters. To get this effect, have the person asking the questions to sit to one side of the camera, then ask your subject to look at that person when answering. In Figure 10-1, we positioned our interviewer to the right side of the camera. This means the subject is always looking into the open space of the frame.

Remind subjects that they can retake the answer if they make a mistake. You can also ask your interviewer to smile, nod, and keep eye contact with the subjects while they're answering questions. This can help them feel more comfortable.

Question in the answer

Before you start filming your interview, ask your subject or character to answer the question fully, and to include the question in the answer. For example, our crew asked their subjects what their role was in the film. If the subject just said "camera operator," this may not make any sense to the audience when the question was cut out later. If instead the answer was "I'm one of the camera operators in this film," then viewers would have no trouble understanding. Your subjects may forget to do this for every question, however, so you may have to remind them from time to time.

Recording Clean Sound

Because you'll be filming the interviews in mid shots or close-up shots, get the microphone fairly close to your subject. If you're using your camera's onboard microphone, you'll have to get the camera as close as you can without creating an extreme close-up shot. If you're using an external microphone, on the other hand, you can position it close to your subject without having to move your camera closer.

It's also a good idea to make sure you avoid as much background noise as possible. It's very important to hear the answers from your subject, and not any distracting noise.

Lavalier microphones are often used when filming interviews. (See Figure 10-2.) These are very small microphones that can be attached to your subject's shirt with a wire connected to a belt pack. These are very useful because they allow you to get the microphone really close to your subject without giving your sound operator arm-ache. They also help reduce background noise.

Throughout recording your interviews it's a good idea to be monitoring the sound through headphones. This helps detect any unwanted background noises and determine whether the volume or gain levels are set too high.

Figure 10-2

Filming Cutaways

Interviews are great for documentaries, but be careful: Sometimes scene after scene of someone just speaking to the camera can be boring. To keep your audience interested, try including *cutaways*. Cutaways are video clips that appear over interviews and voiceovers to help explain a point or to support what the character is saying. Our crew used cutaway footage over the top of their interviews that showed the cast and crew working on their film. This helps the audience see what happened behind the scenes and to show what the subject is explaining during the interview. Cutaway shots can also be used to hide the points in a clip where the subject pauses, says "ums" or "errs," or makes a mistake. (Figure 10-3 shows an example of one of the cutaway shots used in our crew's documentary.)

In the next project, I show you how to place these cutaway video clips over the top of the interviews when editing.

Figure 10-3

Creating the Perfect Ending

As the ending is the last bit of your documentary that your audience will see, it's important to spend time getting it right. Your audience should be able to walk away from your documentary feeling satisfied and informed. To do this, you need to conclude your story and include any answers to questions asked at the beginning. You may want to include:

✔ Any final thoughts or feelings from your subject or characters

✔ Any results from an event

✔ Information about an event or charity

✔ A challenge for your audience

✔ Video footage to support the information

You may also decide to include a voiceover here to summarize and conclude your story or topic. I show you how to record and add voiceovers to your documentary in the next project.

Try It Out Yourself

Are you ready to shoot your documentary? Using the information in this project you can now create an introduction, film interviews, film cutaway shots to go with the interviews, and create an ending to summarize the main points and conclude your documentary.

In the next project, I show you how to add voiceovers and edit your documentary in iMovie.

Overlaying and Underlaying in Editing

Now it's time to bring together the footage you have shot for your documentary (see Project 10) into your editing tool to see how it all works together.

Our crew filmed some behind-the-scenes footage from their short film project. They captured some interviews on the day of filming and also set up interviews with the cast and crew on another day after filming. They're going to use this footage and these interviews (along with a voiceover in the introduction) to create their documentary.

Interviews are a great opportunity to overlay shots related to the topic and to support what the characters are talking about.

Overlaying shots with interviews helps to keep the audience interested and focused on the information being presented. Hopefully you'll have filmed enough extra footage or supporting footage to use as cutaways with the interviews within your documentary. You can never shoot too much supporting footage as it's best to have more to choose from than to have to go out and film more if you don't have enough footage.

In this project, I show you how to overlay footage and underlay a voiceover when editing to make your documentary look even more professional.

Preparing Your Documentary in the Timeline

Before we move on to the first section, follow these steps to make sure your documentary is ready in the timeline to underlay a voiceover and overlay footage:

1. **Open iMovie and create a new event. Name the event with the title of your documentary.**

   If you need a reminder, Project 5 can help guide you through these steps.

2. **Import the footage you wish to use in your documentary into your new event.**

3. **Within your new event, create a new movie project with no theme. Name the movie project with the title of your documentary.**

4. **Select the clips you want to use within the introduction and drag them one at a time into the timeline.**

Aim to drag the clips into the timeline in the order you want them to play in your documentary. This may help you prevent having to change the order later, which can get confusing.

Think carefully about the structure of your introduction because this is an important part of your documentary. The order of your clips should aim to captivate and grab the attention of your audience. Make the clips short and interesting. Remember, the introduction should be a teaser of what is to come in the main section.

When the clips for the introduction to your documentary are together in the timeline, you're ready to move on to recording a voiceover.

Recording a Voiceover

A voiceover can help you tell your story. In fact, you may decide to write your voiceover before filming to help structure your documentary and plan the shots needed. Even so, you may wish to record your voiceover after filming because your structure could change or you may decide to take out or include more information.

Don't worry if you don't have a recording studio in your house — you can record voiceovers on your computer or cellphone. As long as you have a microphone or webcam connected to your computer, iMovie's tool for recording voiceovers will work for you.

Before recording your voiceover, keep in mind these simple ways to improve the quality of the audio recording:

✔ Make sure there is as little background noise as possible around you while recording. Letting people know that you are recording audio may help stop them from interrupting you or making noises in the background.

✔ Check for echoes in the room you're recording in. An echo can be maddening for viewers. You can check for one during filming either by clapping or by saying a word loudly and then listening carefully for any echo. If there is an echo, try another room. Find a room with little to no echo.

✔ Place your mouth six to eight inches away from the microphone when recording, roughly the distance from the end of your thumb to the end of your outstretched little finger.

To record the voiceover using iMovie, follow these steps:

1. **Have your voiceover script ready to read from.**

2. **Move the play head to the point in your timeline where you want to start your voiceover.**

3. **Press the V key on your keyboard to bring up the voiceover recording function, as shown in Figure 11-1.**

Voiceover recording tools

Figure 11-1

If this doesn't work, you can also show the voiceover recording function by choosing Record Voiceover from the Window menu in the top toolbar, as shown in Figure 11-2.

Figure 11-2

4. **Click on the microphone icon to start recording your voiceover, as shown in Figure 11-3.**

After the microphone icon has been pressed, there is a countdown giving you three seconds before recording begins. After that, you can begin your voiceover.

Because you're recording, a red and green strip appears underneath your footage, as shown in Figure 11-4.

5. **Click the microphone icon to stop recording.**

A completed voiceover within a green audio box now appears below your footage, as shown in Figure 11-5.

Microphone icon

Figure 11-3

Figure 11-4

Figure 11-5

The voiceover clip you've just recorded now appears as an audio clip within your event.

6. **You can trim the beginning and end of your voiceover to remove any unwanted sections. To trim your voiceover down, select it, then hover your mouse pointer over the beginning or end of the clip. When you see two arrows appear, click, hold, and drag left or right to make the clip shorter or longer, as needed. (See Figure 11-6.)**

Note that you cannot make the clip longer unless it has been trimmed to be shorter earlier.

If you want to record another voiceover in your timeline, repeat the steps above.

The two-arrow cursor

Figure 11-6

Adding a Voiceover under Your Footage

You can record your voiceover on your cellphone, computer, or your camcorder. Using your camcorder gives you better audio quality than your cellphone or computer because the microphone on your camcorder is better.

To use a voiceover recorded on an external device, follow these steps:

1. **Record the voiceover on your camcorder or external device.**

I find it useful to point the camera at the person doing the voiceover or at the external microphone when recording the sound. This helps you to find the clips when searching through the clips when it comes to importing.

2. **Import the footage or audio clip that the voiceover is recorded on into the event for your documentary.**

Figure 11-7 shows an audio clip being imported from a memory card.

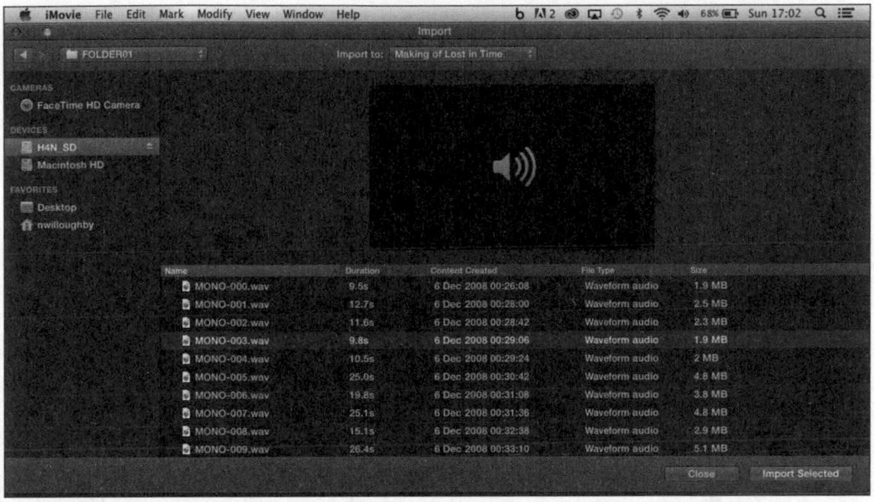

Figure 11-7

3. **Select the part of the voiceover clip you want to use in your timeline.**

   Click, hold, and drag the selected clip under the footage in the timeline to the position you want, as shown in Figure 11-8.

Figure 11-8

If your voiceover is recorded on a video clip, it turns into an audio clip when you drag it under the footage in your timeline. This is because iMovie recognizes that you want to use only the audio of this clip.

Adding Footage over Your Interviews

Adding supporting footage over your interviews can look really great, and it can also be used to cover up the cut points in your main clips. For instance, if you recorded a long interview with a boring subject, you can cut out all the unwanted footage and then overlay supporting footage over the cuts to hide them. If it's done well, your audience will never know the cuts are there.

You can add supporting footage over your interviews by following these steps:

1. **Select the interview you want to use and drag the selected footage into the timeline.**

   You may have several clips for this interview, so edit these to flow together as smoothly as possible.

   Our crew asked each subject two questions, which were filmed using different shot types. The first question was filmed in a mid shot and the second question in a close-up shot. Figure 11-9 shows how these shots look.

2. **Select the part of the video clip you want to use as a cut-away within your interview.**

3. **Click, hold, and drag the selected clip and place it above the interview footage in the timeline, as shown in Figure 11-10.**

   This clip now replaces whatever is at that point in the interview, but you'll still hear the audio from the interview footage.

Figure 11-9

Figure 11-10

The sound in the new cutaway or supporting clip may be distracting and unnecessary. To mute the sound within the cutaway clip above the interview footage, follow these steps:

1. **Select the cutaway or supporting clip above the interview footage.**

2. **Click on the Adjust button in the toolbar above the playback window, as shown in Figure 11-11.**

Figure 11-11

3. **Click on the Volume Adjust button to show the volume options, as shown in Figure 11-12.**

Figure 11-12

4. **Click, hold, and drag the volume slider to the left to reduce the volume to zero percent, as shown in Figure 11-13.**

Figure 11-13

You can now play back the timeline and see how the cutaway or supporting footage looks in the interview. After bringing the volume down to zero percent, there should be no sound from the cutaway or supporting footage.

If you're using supporting footage from the interview (such as, for example, a shot of your interviewee's hands), make sure to try to match the movement of the hands in the supporting footage to the voice in the interview. If your subject's hands are moving when the subject is not speaking, for example, it might look a little strange.

Adding Credits

It's important to thank and honor all the people who have been involved in the making of your documentary, and including credits at the end is a great way to do that. In big-budget movies, the credits often roll for a long time at the end of the film because there are so many people involved in its creation. Next time you watch a movie, pay attention to the credits and see how many roles there are in the film. Obviously, you won't have that many people involved in your film, but it's still important to thank all of those who helped you make it. People love to see their names scrolling in the credits.

To add credits at the end of your documentary, follow these steps:

1. **Scroll to the end of your timeline to where you want to place your credits.**

2. **Click the Titles button, as shown in Figure 11-14.**

   This shows a list of the types of titles available.

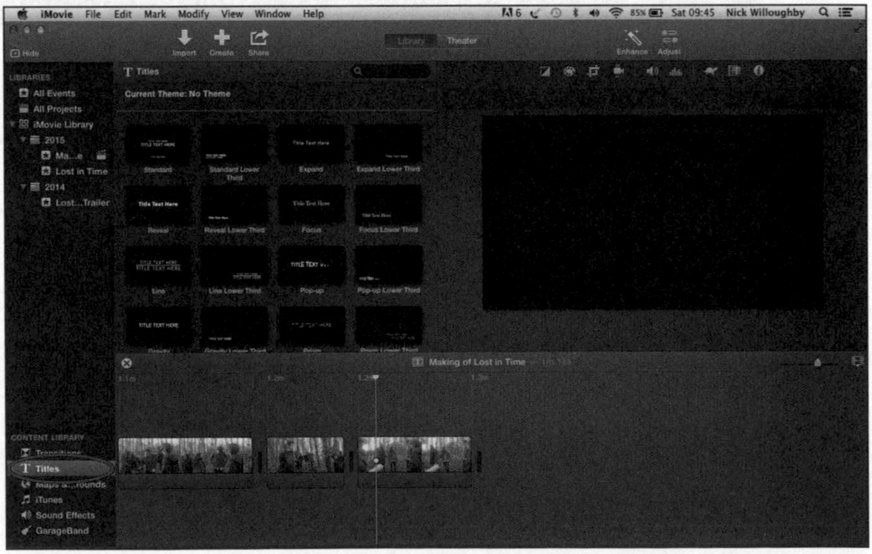

Figure 11-14

3. Scroll down in the Titles window until you see a title called Scrolling Credits, as shown in Figure 11-15.

The Scrolling Credits title

Figure 11-15

4. **Click, hold, and drag the Scrolling Credits title into the time-line after your last shot, as shown in Figure 11-16.**

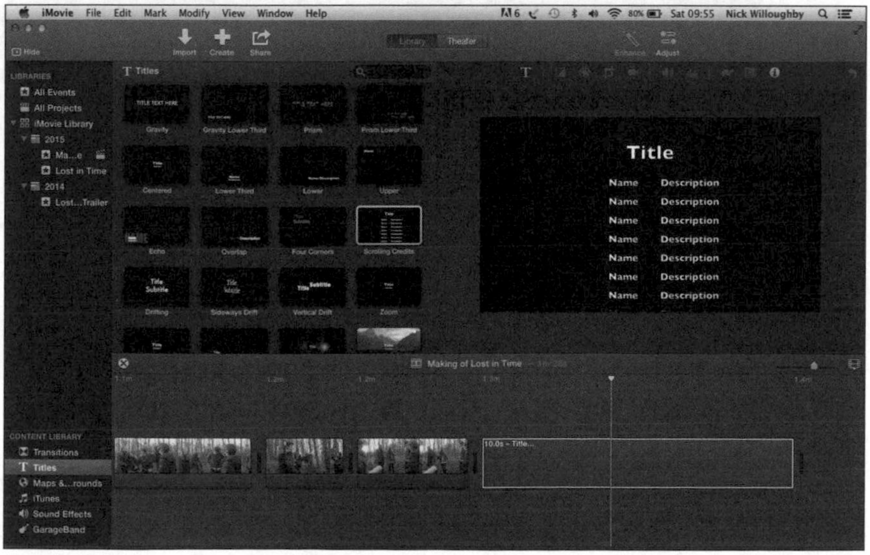

Figure 11-16

The Scrolling Credits title includes the words "Title," "Name," and "Description." This allows you to replace the words with the title of your film, the names of your characters or crew roles, and the names of the actors or crew members.

5. **Double-click on the Scrolling Credits title in the timeline to start entering the details of your film, cast, and crew.**

This highlights the information in the playback monitor window.

6. **Double-click on the word "Title" in the playback monitor window and type in your film's name, as shown in Figure 11-17.**

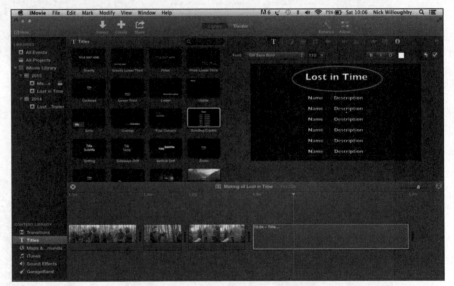

Figure 11-17

7. **Double-click on the word "Name" in the playback window and add the first character or crew role, as shown in Figure 11-18.**

8. **Double-click on the word "Description" in the playback window and add the actor or crew member's name, as shown in Figure 11-19.**

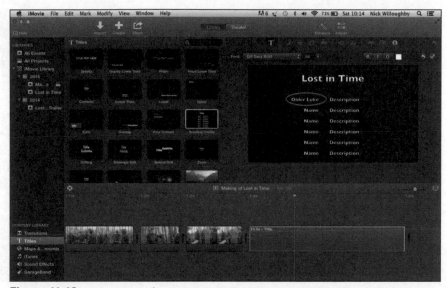

Figure 11-18

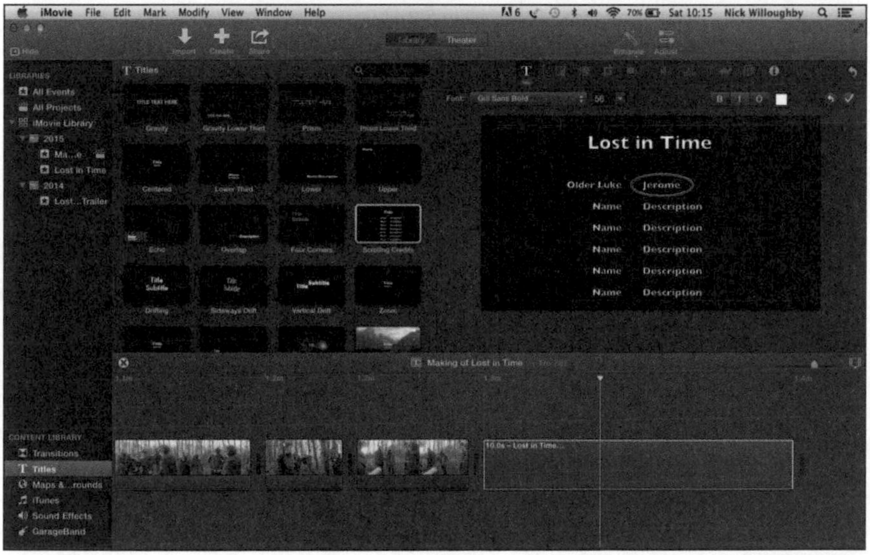

Figure 11-19

9. **After you have entered all cast and crew details, click on the check mark in the right corner above the playback monitor window, as shown in Figure 11-20.**

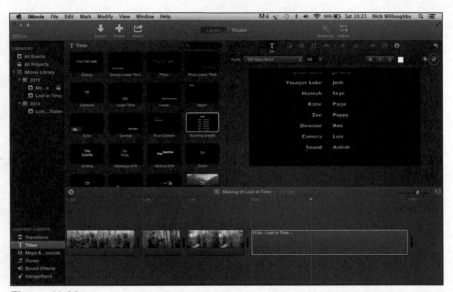

Figure 11-20

10. **You can change the font type by double-clicking on the Scrolling Credits title in the timeline and then select the words that you wish to change by clicking and dragging in the playback monitor window.**

11. **Click open the Font drop-down list above the playback monitor, as shown in Figure 11-21.**

12. **Select the font you want use from the list of fonts available, as shown in Figure 11-22.**

13. **To change the font size, select the text you want to change and click open the Font Size drop-down menu or enter the font size manually, as shown in Figure 11-23.**

Your documentary has now been edited, you can add a voiceover under your footage, and include cutaway shots over your interview footage. All that is left to do now is to export your movie to share. If you need reminding of how to do this, you can revisit Project 5, where I show you how to export to share. You can also upload your documentary to YouTube, which I cover in Project 8.

Figure 11-21

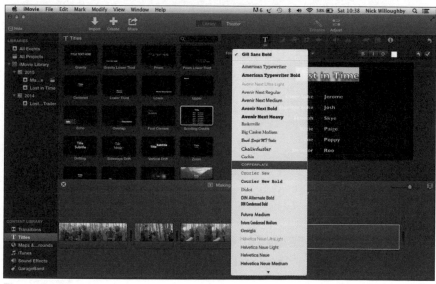

Figure 11-22

Figure 11-23

Week 4
Creating Your First Short Narrative Film

This week you'll . . .

To see the short film our young film crew made, visit www.dummies.com/extras/ digitalfilmmakingforkids. There you can also find a video offering some tips on location-hunting and on working with your actors.

Assembling Your Film Crew

"Many hands make light work." "Two heads are better than one." You know these sayings. They're clichés, but they're also true. By assembling a film crew, you can split your workload and focus on the quality of your film.

Hundreds of people are normally involved in big-budget films, but you don't have to recruit anywhere near that number. Two or more people will make a difference. The number of people I have on set depends on the size of the film project and how complex the scene is. For smaller projects, the crew may be just myself and one other person. For bigger projects, on the other hand, I might call in ten or more people to help. Sometimes you don't want loads of crew helping because you're filming in a tight space or you simply don't need that many people around.

Filmmaking is a team activity. You need people around to help, whether it be with creating ideas, writing scripts, drawing storyboards, or helping with the filming or editing. Building a team around you is important because you can call on people with different skills to help and share the responsibility of making a film. Filmmaking is simply harder to do on your own.

In this project, I show you the roles involved in making films and what they do. Armed with this information, you can decide whom you want to invite to help make your film.

Who Can Help?

When you tell people that you're making a film, you'll get many offers to help. This is great, but you want to choose only the people who'll help you make your film. You don't want those who just want to do it for a laugh.

You may also find that most of the people who want to be involved in your film want to act. If I had a dollar for the number of times someone wanted to act in one of my films, I'd probably be a millionaire. I find it easier to choose the actors for my film after the film has been written and after I've chosen my crew. You may want to ask your crew to help cast or audition the actors for your film. If you want to act in your film, you'll have to choose people who will be happy to film.

When considering whom to invite to help with you film, think about the sorts of people with whom you work well. It's important to have a range of characters and personalities in your group who won't clash. The people I work with to make films are very different from me, but this is a good thing. I don't want to have too many other people like me around. I'm good at coming up with ideas and writing stories, but I'm not always great at organizing the filming and completing projects. This is why I have people around me who are good at taking the ideas I come up with and organizing the filming. If I had people like me around me, there would be loads of ideas and no finished films. You may find that you are great with the technical side of filmmaking and enjoy working with the cameras, so you may need people around you who will help to come up with ideas and help with creating the story.

Another thing to think about is the kinds of equipment you'll need. You may have people around you who have equipment that they would like to use to help make your film. If your friend has a camera he or she is happy to let you use for your film, consider making that friend the camera operator.

Roles in a Team

There are so many different roles in filmmaking. You can see this when you watch the credits at the end of a mainstream film: The credits seem to go on for ages at the end of a film as they thank all the people involved, from the actors to the costume designers.

The following list describes some of the main roles in making a film. You don't have to fill every role with your film, of course, but these are your possibilities:

- **Writer:** The person who writes the story and script for filming. The writer is really involved at the start of the filmmaking process, but occasionally he or she can be invited to be on set when filming.

- **Executive producer:** The person who provides the money and support to make the film. Films cost a lot of money, so without executive producers, many films wouldn't be made.

- **Producer:** The person responsible for organizing the production and filming from start to finish. Some of the duties of a producer include working with writers, the director, and the cast to prepare the script ready for shooting; organizing and managing the film crew; planning and scheduling the shoot;

reviewing the edits with the director; and organizing the distribution of the final film.

- **Production manager:** The person who works with the executive producer to organize the people needed to make the film.

- **Director:** Directors work with the actors and crew during filming to tell the story and to get the best result for the audience. They also help to refine the story and script before filming and review the edits during post-production.

- **Assistant directors:** The person who works with the director to organize the crew and actors and to make sure everything is running smoothly during filming.

- **Director of photography:** The person who works with the camera and lighting crew to make the shots look great. They also work with the director to decide on what types of shots to use. In small productions, sometimes the director of photography is the camera operator.

- **Location scout:** The person who decides on the locations to use for each scene before filming. They spend a lot of time travelling around looking at potential locations for films.

- **Casting director:** The person who auditions the actors to play the characters in the film. They have to sit through a lot of auditions to make sure that the person they choose for a role in a film is the right one.

- **Camera operator:** The camera operator is responsible for filming and setting up the camera shots for each scene.

- **Boom operator/sound mixer:** The person responsible for holding the microphone and recording sound on set. The boom operator also monitors the sound during filming to check for volume levels and any sound issues or background noises.

✔ **Gaffer:** Gaffers work with the director of photography or camera operator to set up lighting for each scene.

✔ **Key grip:** Key grips are responsible for much of the equipment used in filming, including tripods, dollies, cranes, lighting, and so on.

✔ **Props master:** The person responsible for finding props needed for each scene. Some props need to be designed and built for a scene and others can be bought.

✔ **Makeup and hair:** The person responsible for actors' makeup and hair on the set. Often simple makeup is needed to stop shine on the face from the lights, but sometimes more complicated makeup is needed to create an effect.

✔ **Costume designer:** The person responsible for the clothes worn by actors on set. The costume designer will have to obtain clothes based on the character played by the actor and sometimes will have to create costumes for a character.

✔ **Actors:** These are the people who play the characters in the film. They take advice from the directors to bring the character to life using the dialogue written in the script.

✔ **Editor:** Editors are responsible for placing the footage together in the editing tool to tell the story. They often work to make sure the director is happy with the final result.

✔ **Craft service:** This is the department responsible for providing food and drinks for the cast and crew. This is an important role and one easily forgotten when organizing a film shoot.

Your Role

As a filmmaker, your role is to organize and motivate your team and use their skills to create your film. You may choose to act or direct, but you're still responsible for your team.

Everyone is different and everyone has different strengths and skills. You may be wondering what role you'll take within the team. To help you, I have divided the roles to suit different character types in the following list:

- ✔ **Creative:** As the name suggests, creative people like to create things. They are likely to have more energy, be motivated, expressive, imaginative, and possibly say how they feel. A creative person will enjoy story and script writing, acting, directing, location scouting, prop hunting, and editing. He or she may also want to be involved in everything, so you may have to help a creative person choose.

- ✔ **Technical:** Technical people usually enjoy using the equipment and learning how things work. They enjoy problem-solving and can concentrate on fine detail for longer periods of time. Technical people enjoy camera operating, sound operating, being a gaffer or key grip, and editing. Technical people are our friends; they can do amazing things.

  You may have noticed that editing is included in both creative and technical roles. This is because editing uses technical skills to build the film in the timeline and to add effects, and also the creative skills necessary to make judgments about what will bring the story to life.

- ✔ **Manager:** People who fit into the manager category usually like to organize things, or put them into order. They have a spreadsheet for everything; they're good with people; and they know how to get the best out of the people they work with. Managers enjoy directing and assisting, being a producer, being a production manager, or a casting director. If you want something done, ask a manager.

The categories described above are only general, of course, but they should help you assign roles to people in your team. All the people described in that list need each other to make the filmmaking process work and to complete a project.

Building a Team

People like to be given responsibilities. If you assign a role to a member of your team, that person will naturally feel responsible for that role and want to do the best he or she can. It's good to remind that person of the importance of that role and to offer encouragement from time to time.

In your team, you may be working with friends. If you're working with someone you don't know, however, you may likely become friends over the course of making your film. I've made loads of friends through making films because you meet people with similar interests. Sometimes the only downside to working with friends is that friends can distract you easily and harm your focus on getting the film made. Don't worry, I've been there. When I first started making films, I'd spend more time laughing with my team than making the film. This wasn't good for progress. I soon discovered that it was better to strike a balance: I could have a laugh as long as I quickly got back to the task at hand.

When you build your team, make sure each member is comfortable with the role he or she has been given, and that all of them know what they're doing and what's expected of them. Training may be needed to develop skills and teamwork, and the best way to do this is to go out and film. You may also want to ask your crew to buy and read this book so they understand some of the technical language you're using and the finer details of what you're asking them to do.

Try It Out Yourself

Now it's time to build your team. First, think about your role within the team. Will you be directing, acting, or filming? After you've decided this, you can build your team around you with the roles that you need to make your film. In the next project, you start to work on creating your first short film with your new team.

Telling Your Story

Story is essential to your film. We live in a world of stories. We experience stories every day. Everyone loves a good story, but coming up with an idea for a story can be the hardest part of writing a film.

I like to think that we have a creative muscle in our brain. We don't, of course, but I like to think we do. I also think that the more we use that imaginary creative muscle, the more we can come up with fresh and fantastic ideas. Look at the world around you. You are surrounded by ideas and themes and stories, all waiting to inspire a film.

When I'm thinking of ideas, I like to get fresh air, maybe a bit of exercise. I find that fresh air and exercise help me clear my thoughts and allow me to explore the creative caves of my mind. Try going for a walk or perhaps just outside. If you must stay indoors, be sure to turn off distractions like the TV and your smartphone. You may also want to meet up with your team to discuss ideas together — in groups, ideas often bounce off each other. One idea may spark another, better idea in someone else.

Our film crew came up with the idea for their story in this way, through discussing ideas as a group. They decided on the thriller genre fairly quickly, and then came up with the idea of children lost in a forest. They wanted to include a creepy character that the children meet in the forest and try to run away from, and from there, the story just came together.

Don't expect ideas to come instantly. It can take a while to think of an idea that can be used to create a story. It's a good idea to write down every idea you come up with, even if you think it's not great. When you come back to that idea later, it may inspire a better idea.

In this chapter, I explain what makes a good story and show you how to transform your ideas into a fantastic story for your short film.

What Makes a Good Story?

Have you ever thought about why your favorite film is your favorite film? Is it the actors? Is it the special effects? Or is it the story? A good story is made up of a beginning, middle, and end. This is also known as a three-act structure. Without these three sections, the audience may feel confused or as if they have missed something.

Before writing a story, you need to develop the idea. (For more about creating an idea, see Project 6.) If you're short of ideas, consider using the idea you created for your trailer as the basis for your film, which is what our young film crew did.

When developing your idea, decide on a genre for your film, then think about what your audience would want to see. Is there an existing story you can base your idea on? Think about what's possible to film with the resources, actors, and locations you have. Remember to write down all your ideas — and keep in mind, no idea is a bad idea.

When I'm writing a story for a film, I begin with dividing my idea into a beginning, middle, and end. This helps me to structure the story and work out if something is missing or doesn't work.

Act I: The Setup

This is where you set up your story, characters, and genre, revealing any background information or character history that's essential to the story. You don't have to jump straight in to introducing your characters at the beginning of Act I, but it should be done at some point in the first act. It's important to keep this section engaging as your audience could turn away if nothing happens. You may want to build up to the main event and confrontation. Act one in our crew's film includes the children meeting in the forest and introducing the characters and setting. Our crew build up to the main event with the children finding themselves lost. At this point, the audience has no idea what is coming and about to happen to them, but the tension is building.

Act II: The Confrontation

This is normally the longest section and can be the hardest to write. This section is where you introduce the main event or the confrontation. Here, there should be a turning point in your story. Maybe your characters are in danger. Maybe there's an unexpected twist in your story. It's your opportunity to grab the attention of your audience or surprise them with a story twist.

In our crew's film, Act II starts with the children in the forest discovering that someone is following them. Over the course of the act, our crew builds up the tension and panic in the characters until the unexpected twist: The characters find a time vortex in the forest, and at the same time, they meet the character that has been following them, a man from the future who turns out to be one of the children, all grown up. He explains that he wants to save the children by helping them out of the forest.

Act III: The Resolution

This is where you bring your story to an end — but remember to keep things interesting. You can always introduce another plot twist here to grab the attention of your audience. Your resolution shows how your characters deal with and overcome the conflict in Act II. This might be the most emotional part of your film.

In our crew's film, Act III shows how the children try to get out of the forest before it gets dark. It's a race against time, which adds emotion and tension for the audience. Our crew ends their film with the children finding their way out of the forest and ultimately changing their future and saving everyone.

You don't always have to have a happy ending. You could write an unexpected ending as long as it makes sense to your audience and won't leave them wondering what's just happened. It's important to take your audience on an "emotional rollercoaster," meaning that your story takes your audience's emotions up and down throughout the film. If you just have lots of action all the way through, and no resting moments, your audience will feel emotionally exhausted and perhaps even bored.

Your audience will follow the emotions of your characters, so try to include a range of emotions and feelings in your story. If one moment your characters are scared because they can hear noises in the forest, and the next, they're running because they're being chased, and the moment after that, they're upset because they realize they're in danger, this will keep your audience interested and engaged.

Another way to keep your audience interested is by being unpredictable with your story. Don't be too unpredictable or create an event or situation out of nowhere to fix a problem in your story, however, because you may confuse your audience. Still, including an unexpected twist in your story could make your film great, as long as it fits in with the rest of the story.

Creating Your Characters

Characters are essential to a film because they tell the story through what they do and say. Audiences may not realize it but they build relationships with the characters in a film: They either love them or hate them. It's good to have characters that are different from each other because it adds to the realism of your film.

When writing your story, it's a good idea to think carefully about your characters and to create a profile for each of them. Big-budget films and TV shows spend ages developing the characters before writing the scripts because understanding the character helps writers decide what the character will say or how the character will react to a situation. It's also useful for the actors to read their character's profile in order for them to better assume that character's persona when acting and to know how to deliver the dialogue.

It's also important to keep all your characters different from each other. When your characters are too alike, your story won't be very interesting. You may want to have one of your characters more worried than the others, one who's brave, or one who's quieter than the others. In our crew's story, they created the characters to be very different from each other, and they wrote a profile for each character in their film. (See Figure 13-1.)

Character Profiles

Luke (Younger)
Luke is quieter than the others. He seems happy to enter the forest and not worried until they get lost. When they find the vortex he seems interested and wants to explore. He follows the rest of the group and is not very confident.

Luke (Older)
Older Luke appears to be angry and aggressive but he is just protecting the group. He will do anything to stop them going into the forest. Older Luke is determined but very weak. He is also confused, as he has spent most of his life lost in the forest.

Zoe
Zoe is the second oldest member of the group. She is confident and the leader of the group. Others look up to her, which is why they all follow her into the forest. At first she is not worried but when they start getting lost, she starts to get more and more worried. She soon becomes the weaker one of the group when they start hearing noises

Katie
Katie is the oldest of the group. She is a little nervous at first but is happy

---

Figure 13-1

Your Story on One Page

Before writing your story it's a good idea to write your story on one page. This is called a *synopsis.* A synopsis is an outline of the story, which can be used to describe your film to others.

For big Hollywood films, a synopsis is often used to explain the film to potential investors. After the film is released, the synopsis is used to help sell and advertise it. If you look on the back of a DVD case, you'll see a short version of the synopsis, which gives viewers a brief summary of the film.

The synopsis you create, however, will be used to finalize your story outline and to help to write your script. It can also help you see whether your story makes sense to others. You may wish to show your synopsis to other people before you write the script.

I always pass my film ideas by my family and friends before I write my scripts. These are the people who care about me and want to help me, so I can rely on them to be honest about my ideas.

Scene Selection

A *scene selection* or *scene list* outlines all the scenes within a film. This list breaks down the film into sections and scenes, and is used to see how the story flows and whether scenes should be added or taken away. Creating a scene list gives the filmmaker a good overview and outline of the film.

Using your one-page story synopsis, you can create a list of scenes in your film. You can divide your story into scenes when there is a change in place or time. If you start your film in the kitchen of a home and then want to change to the park, that is a new scene. If you start your film in the kitchen and then want to move to later that day in the same kitchen, that is also a new scene.

Creating a list of scenes in your film will help you understand what locations, props, and actors you need. Note that a scene list is different than a shot list because a scene list simply lists the scenes in your film to depict the flow of the story. This helps you see whether anything is missing or unnecessary in your story. Since each scene in a short film can be expected to be between two and three minutes in length, on average, a scene list can also give you an idea of how long your finished film will be. A more precise calculation of length can be made when writing the script. (Figure 13-2 shows the scene list our crew made for their film.)

When creating your list of scenes, include for each the scene number, the scene name, and a description. This information helps to match the scenes in the script. From the description you can see how the story flows and whether it's missing anything.

Scene List

Project Name: __Lost in Time__

Production Company: __Filmmaking For Kids__

Scene No.	Scene Name	Description
1	Waiting for their friends	Friends meet and decide to go into forest.
2	Enter the Forest	Shots of the group walking through forest
3	Hide and seek	Group playing games – decide to go home
4	Lost	The group realize they are lost – They start hearing noises
5	The Shadow	The group see someone following them – scream and run.
6	The Portal	The group stumble across portal and meet stranger – run away

Figure 13-2

Writing the Script

I love writing scripts because it's the moment when your characters start coming to life. If you've created a scene list and character profiles, writing the script is easy: It's just a matter of explaining what happens in each scene by using the dialogue from your characters. Your script should include:

✔ **Action/direction:** This refers to descriptions of anything happening on-screen besides character dialogue. You can include shot information and notes for filming here, too.

✔ **Character names:** Include a character's name before his or her lines of dialogue so your actors know who's speaking.

✔ **Dialogue:** This is the words spoken by the characters in your script. This should be written as naturally as possible.

Figure 13-3 shows how our crew's script was written and arranged. They used software called Celtx, which you can download for free from www.celtx.com. There are many other script-writing tools available to use as well, or you can just use any word processing application to do the same job.

```
SCENE 1 - EXT. WAITING FOR THEIR FRIENDS

Zoe and Hannah are standing at the entrance to the forest
waiting for their friends to arrive. As they are talking
Luke and Katy turn up.

                    ZOE
          You ready to go?

                    KATIE
          Are you sure we should go in?

                    HANNAH
          Yeah, let's just go!

They walk out of shot.


SCENE 2 - EXT. ENTER THE FOREST

The group walk through the forest talking to each other
and laughing. Hannah and Luke are throwing leaves at the
others. As they walk through the forest they are looking
up at the tall trees. POV shot of the trees.


SCENE 3 - HIDE AND SEEK
```

Figure 13-3

Writing Dialogue

Dialogue is simply a conversation between your characters. The key behind writing good dialogue is to make it sound natural. When writing dialogue, I always try to imagine what I would say if I were the characters speaking. Then I read my dialogue out loud to see whether it sounds natural. If you stumble over a word or find a line hard to read, then look for an easier way of saying it. Dialogue can always change; you may find that your actors naturally find an easier way of saying the same thing in their own way. This is okay as long as they don't change the meaning of the dialogue.

You don't have to use dialogue to explain all the things in your story. Remember, film is an audio and video medium, so you can use facial expressions, body language, or actions to express how a character feels or to tell your story. I made a film called "Remember Me" that has no dialogue at all: We used a mixture of facial expressions, music, and imagery to tell the story.

14 Location Hunting and Props

Good locations and props can make your film look great. Finding the right locations and props for your film is important, but it's not always as easy as it may seem.

Many of the locations in Hollywood films are stages and sets built in large studios. They do this so that they can have control over the location and so they don't have to worry about closing off roads and public places. Of course, they have the money to do this, but as low-budget filmmakers we have to find real locations to use.

Props are any items or objects in the film that are used by the actors or that appear in the scenes. Imagine organizing all the props for a blockbuster film — it would take ages! This is why

they have props departments: entire departments devoted to supplying props for the film. The props department uses the script to work out what props are needed in the film and then creates or finds those props.

Costumes are the clothes worn by the characters in the film. Again, large-scale films use costume departments to create or find the costumes needed for the film.

When writing your film, you may want to think about the locations, props, and costumes that are available to you. This will help prevent problems when it's time to begin filming. Setting one of your scenes on top of the Eiffel Tower in Paris, for instance, may cause problems unless you live very close and can get permission. Setting your film in the 1800s may cause problems when looking for locations, props, and costumes.

In this chapter, I show you how to find the locations, props, and costumes to make your film look great.

Finding the Right Locations for Your Film

Locations for mainstream films are normally found by a *location scout,* whose job is to use the script to find buildings, fields, forests, and other locations that suit the scenes in a film.

How simple can you make a location? This is one of the first things you should think about when location hunting. If your scene is set on top of the Eiffel Tower, does it have to be there? Could the scene take place somewhere else — like, say, your back garden?

The next thing to think about is whether the location works for the scene and the story. If you're filming a scene where the dialogue and emotions are important, you may want to find a location with few distractions, one that will help build emotions. Our crew chose a forest for their film because someone could get easily lost in forest. A forest also has few distractions apart from the occasional person walking his or her dog.

It's good to keep the locations for your film close to where you live. This makes it so much easier to film your scenes. Most of the scenes in my films are based in locations in the village where I live. There shouldn't be any need to travel too far unless you can't find a location near you, at which point you should speak to your parents nicely and ask them to drive you there. One of the reasons I use locations near me is because when I'm out filming, people recognize me and know what I'm doing. (See the next section, "Do You Have Permission?")

After you've decided on the locations you need for your film, you can go out and find them. You may decide to use rooms in your house or your back garden, which is great. When you go out location hunting, remember to take a still camera with you. It's good to photograph the location for use when planning your shots. Photographing the location also shows you what it looks like through a lens. Some locations can look different on a camera than in real life. (See Figure 14-1.)

Figure 14-1

It helps to visit and photograph your location at the time of day you are planning to film. This can help you work out where the natural light is coming from. If your location has a specific background you want to use, you will need to consider the best time of day to capture it in the best light.

Be sure to have a Plan B for your location. What would happen if you arrive at your location to film your scene and find that people are camping there or having a party? You can either find another day to film or have a second location planned. For one of my short films, I found the perfect location for a forest scene, but when I turned up there, a woodcutter was using a chainsaw in the forest and we couldn't hear a word the actors were saying. Luckily, I planned a second location, which turned out to be just as good (maybe even better) than the first.

Do You Have Permission?

When you film your scenes you're likely to attract attention from passersby. Sometimes people quietly walk by having a sneaky look, sometimes they stop and watch, and sometimes they walk by shouting things as loudly as they can. People may ask you what you're doing and sometimes may ask if you have permission to film. This is one of the downsides to making films. Most of the time, however, you won't have anyone bothering you.

If you find a location you like, it's important to check that you're allowed to film there. If it's someone's property, you'll need the owner's permission. If it's a public place, you may need to ask your local authority. When filming, make sure you avoid getting other people in the shot. If you do, you'll need to get a permission form signed by them. This is why I use locations that I know and that are local to me: I already have contacts that I can get permission from.

Getting permission to film people is really important because the last thing you want is to have to worry about someone you've filmed changing his or her mind and demanding to be taken out of your film, especially after you've completed your edit. To avoid this, ask the people who appear in your film to complete a model release form. By signing this, they are agreeing that you can use their image in your film, and after they sign it, they give up their right to change their minds about it later. I use a standard model release form, a blank version of which is available for you to download at this book's companion website.

I always find that people are happy to let you film on or in their property if you ask them. For some locations I use friend's houses, and I always give them a box of chocolates for letting me use their house. For one shoot, I filmed in a friend's house for over a week while my friend was away on holiday. (I got permission to film first, of course.) This was ideal: The house was empty, and we could take over the house without causing any disruption to my friend's life.

When the owner of a location has agreed to let you use it, make sure you both also agree on a date to film. This allows the owner to make sure that nothing else is happening on that day at that location.

Choosing Props and Costumes

When it comes to low-budget filmmaking, props and costumes are usually afterthoughts: They're not even considered until it's time to begin filming. Still, it pays to plan ahead. You don't want to have to scramble at the last minute for an important prop.

If you're setting your story in the current year, obtaining props and costumes is much easier. If you set your story in the past or the future, however, you're a brave soul: You'll probably have a hard time finding the appropriate props and costumes. For this reason, I tend to keep my films set in the current year.

A simple way to organize costumes for your film is to use the clothes your actors are already wearing. Just ask them to bring a few changes of clothes if you want to film other scenes. I like to avoid advertising clothing brands so I ask the actors to bring clothes without logos or brand names on them. This avoids any possible disagreements with large clothing companies over copyright laws. You may want to suggest the types of clothes that your actors wear. If you're filming a scene in which they need to dress up, for example, you can ask them to bring smart clothes. If you're filming a scene in which the actors stand in mud, on the other hand, you can ask them to wear clothes that they won't mind getting dirty. If your actors don't have clothes they'll let get dirty, you can always buy some cheap T-shirts or find clothes for them in charity shops.

Clothing and costumes always seem to cause the most continuity problems, as when one of your characters magically has an item of clothing appear or disappear halfway through a scene. This normally occurs when you take a break halfway through filming a scene and your actor takes off (or puts on) a coat, scarf, gloves, or jumper. When you start filming again, often no one notices the difference, and then later your editor has a heart attack trying to make all the pieces fit. Look out for continuity issues when filming, and make sure your actors know that they need to be careful about removing or adding items of clothing.

Props often can be more difficult to find than clothing, depending on what you're looking for. If you're filming in your house and the scene is based in a house, then you may not need to find any props at all — you can just use what's already in the house. (Make sure you get permission from your parents or from the owner of the house to film there, and check whether they're okay with their furniture appearing in your film.) If you need to find specific props for your film, ask people you know if they have what you need, or look on eBay. You're likely to find anything you need on eBay.

Try It Out Yourself

Now it's time to go through your script and make a list of all the locations, props, and costumes you'll need. Go out and find the locations and make sure they're available for the day of filming. Obtain all necessary permissions. Ask your actors to bring clothes or try and find any costume items or props that you don't have.

In the next project, I show you how to choose actors to play the characters in your film.

Choosing Actors for Your Film

Your actors are the face of your film; they take the story and dialogue you created and bring it to life through their performances. This is why a good actor can make a film — and a bad actor can break one.

When looking for an actor, you are looking for someone who will take on a character in your film and perform the lines with feeling and realism. Your audiences need to believe everything your actors say, and they need to believe they're real.

When you wrote your film, you may have had someone in mind to play the characters. Some writers base their characters on an

actor they have in mind, and some directors prefer to work with certain actors regularly because they're comfortable with those actors and understand how to work with them.

As I said before, many people will offer to act in your film, but it's important that you choose your actors carefully. Your film is your creation, it's important to you, and you don't want to let it down with a poor cast. You may want to act in your film, which is fine, but you will need to choose someone to direct your film whom you trust and whom you know will work well with you.

In this chapter, I show you how to choose actors to play the characters in your film and how to get the best from them.

Running Auditions

Let's say you have a queue of people fighting over the main part in your film, and you're wondering whom you should choose. Well, running auditions is the answer. Auditions are a great way to give your potential cast the opportunity to show how good they are and why they deserve a part in your film. (See Figure 15-1.)

You may want to ask someone else to run the auditions with you. This allows you to discuss each audition with another person and gives you someone to help you make your decision. I find it's also useful to film the audition: You can watch it again later and remind yourself how well each audition went. It's easy to forget, especially after seeing many actors.

Auditions can be quite stressful, so they're also a good way to see how an actor works under pressure. This can give you an idea of how the actor will behave in front of a camera. After all, even the most confident people can go shy when a camera is pointed at them. Auditions can also be a good experience for the actor, especially if acting is something he or she wants to do as a career.

Figure 15-1

The following list describes some things to look for in the actors you meet when running auditions:

- **How do they deal with stress?** It's not unusual for actors to get nervous. It's how they deal with that problem on-camera that's important. Can they hide their nerves? Do the nerves affect their performance? Do they look like a stunned rabbit in headlights? Give them time to relax by telling them about what will happen in the audition and a bit about the production, if you want. Here you can see how they listen and if they are interested in what you are telling them.

- **Are they natural?** When an actor is performing, does it look and feel real? You should be able to believe what the actor is saying and almost forget that she is playing a role. Does she sound like she is just reading lines? If so, ask her to think more closely about the lines she is performing and to try to imagine herself as the character.

✔ **What's the actor's voice like?** An actor's voice should suit the character and the lines he or she will be saying in the film. When performing, does the actor sound like a robot or does he deliver the lines with feeling and emotion? An actor's voice is as important as his facial expressions and his body. It should convey emotion, and it should sound interesting, not boring. Also, listen to how clear his voice is: Does he mumble or rush words?

✔ **How does the actor respond to direction?** The actors you choose should listen to you and do what you ask them to do. The last thing you want is an actor who thinks she knows better than you and does whatever she likes. During the audition, ask your actors to change something about the way they deliver their performance. See whether they do what you ask (or whether they at least try). You could ask them to pause before saying a line or change the amount of emotion in a line — for example, as the actor to "be more angry," or "be less cheerful."

✔ **How does the actor work with other actors?** It's important that your actors be able to work well both on their own and with other actors. The only way to test this in an audition is to have the actor act a scene with another actor in the audition. Look to see whether the actor responds to what other actor is doing in the scene. Does he overpower the other actor or does he support her?

✔ **Has the actor learned the lines?** If you asked the actor to learn a scene or part of the script for the audition, she should have taken the time to learn it. This shows whether she is committed to your film and is a reflection of how much she wants the part. You could allow her to have the script on hand to refer to, if necessary, but I find that a script can be more of a distraction than a support — if it's there, she'll look at it. Ask her if she's all right with working without a script before taking it away from her.

✏ **What does the actor know about the character?** I love it when actors come in to an audition having done research on me, the film project, and the character they are auditioning for. This shows enthusiasm and a real desire to get the role. As part of your audition process, ask the actor questions about the character and what he knows about the film. Remember, he won't be a mind reader, so unless you provided information about the project with the audition information, then he won't be able to answer much. You could ask him about the character, however, because he could get some information from the script. For example, you could ask him what he thinks is happening in the scene he's prepared, about the emotions the character is expressing, and how he feels about playing the character.

When organizing your audition, make sure as many people as possible know about it so plenty of people turn up. Put an ad in the local newspaper or post one to Craigslist. Create a poster to put up at your school or send text messages to your friends or any other people you think might be interested. Be sure you include the date, time, and location of the audition, along with details about the film and any relevant information about the characters you're auditioning for. It's also good to have people contact you to arrange a time for the audition so you won't have everyone turn up at once. Doing this also gives you an idea of the number of people interested.

Ask the actors to prepare a monologue to perform at the audition. This could be a short play or sketch they can perform on their own. Alternatively, send them a script to learn. The script should be only a few minutes long: You want to see how well the actor performs a character, not how well he or she learns a script. When I audition actors, I like to choose a section of the script from the film. I ask the actors to learn this short script and come ready to perform. If another character is in the script, I'll either read those lines or ask someone else to act the scene with the actor. This can show you how well he or she works with other actors.

Don't feel bad about auditioning people for the roles in your film; it's the best way to choose the right actors. It may be hard to audition people you know — even harder if they don't get the part they want — but you have to do what's best for your film. When you must turn down a friend, remember to explain to him or her why you chose someone else for the part. Make sure you do this carefully and sensitively — there are always nice ways to say things. Perhaps you could say, "You're not exactly what we need for this role," or maybe, "You're better suited for another role in this film."

When looking for actors for your film, sometimes it's worth asking any drama students in your school or drama students from local colleges if they'd like to be involved. For serious students, any work they get is valuable experience — and another film they can add to their portfolio. In some of my first films, I was even able to cast professional actors, who agreed to take part in my film for free as long as I would give them copies of the shots they were in. The actors could use these shots for their portfolio and showreel.

Rehearsing Your Scenes

When you have chosen your actors, start rehearsing with them as soon as possible. Rehearsals are important — it's an opportunity for the actors and the director to develop the characters and to see how the dialogue sounds. It can also be a good time to make any necessary changes to the script.

I like to film the rehearsals because doing so allows me to see how the scenes look on-camera and allows the actors to watch themselves on-screen. This can help the actors learn lines and to make changes to the way they play the characters.

The more rehearsals you run before filming, the better the final result. Don't rush the rehearsals — rehearse a scene each time you meet and only move on to the next scene when you're happy with the one before. Rehearsals make filming easier because the actors will arrive confident with their lines and their character. Running rehearsals improves the quality of your final film.

Getting the Best from Your Actors

During filming, your actors are your best friends — it's important to build a good relationship with them. You need to be able to trust them, and they need to be able to trust you.

Encourage your actors and praise them every time they do something well. Try not to add pressure on them during filming because this will show in their performance. Directors who rush scenes can stress out their actors, who'll forget lines or make mistakes.

When directing your actors, give them clear instructions to help them get into their character. Explain what you want from the actor and describe how you'd like his or her character to react to the situation in a scene. For example: "Imagine you're being chased through a forest and your character is scared by the noise in the trees," or "Your character is not scared by anything and is only interested in the strange time vortex she's found."

By working with your actors and helping them develop their characters in rehearsals, you'll get the best from them, which will ultimately benefit the quality of your film. Also, you need to know your actors. Spending more time with them in rehearsals will allow you to get to know them better and to understand how they work. When filming, you may find that some actors perform their best takes on the first take, especially if they know their lines. Other actors may take a few takes to warm up and will give you a better performance on their last take. The first few takes of a shoot are always hard for actors because they tend to be nervous. When shooting a movie, I usually film the wide shots first, which gives the actors more time to warm up and become more comfortable.

Try It Out Yourself

Have you got any actors in mind or will you need to audition for the roles in your film? When auditioning, remember to provide the actors with a section of the script that you would like them to learn or ask them to prepare a monologue to perform during the audition. When you have chosen your actors, start working and rehearsing with them as soon as possible to help develop their character and get to know them and how they work as this will help to get the best from them when filming.

In the next project, I show you how to develop storyboards for your film to plan your shots and be ready for filming.

Planning Your Shots with a Storyboard

Storyboarding your film is not essential, but it can save you a lot of time and make the filming process much easier. It also allows you to see what your film looks like before you even start filming. Storyboards are a series of images or a written list of scenes normally created before filming to show the crew the types of shots to film in a scene.

Storyboards are a way for the filmmaker to put what's in his or her mind onto paper to show how he or she sees the sequence of shots within a scene being framed and working together.

Without a storyboard, filming on-location can be more complicated and may take longer because the director will have to

Project Name	LOST IN TIME	Production Co.	FILMMAKING FOR KIDS
Scene	1	Page Number	1

1

Shot Type: Wide shot

Description: Zoe and Hannah are standing at the entrance to the forest.

2

Shot Type: Close up / 2 shot.

Description: Zoe and Hannah are talking and look over to see Luke and Katy.

choose the shots on the day of shooting, while the cast and crew wait around. With a prepared storyboard, filming can begin as soon as everything is set up. A storyboard also helps make sure that the director doesn't miss any shots. From the storyboard, a shot list can be created to ensure that all shots are captured on the day of filming.

I use storyboard software, which makes creating storyboards quicker and simpler for bigger projects, but simple hand-drawings can also be fine as long as they're clear enough for the crew to understand.

In this chapter, I show you how to create your own storyboards to impress your crew when filming.

Create a Storyboard

Some people who work in the film industry create storyboards as a full-time job. Their storyboards look like pieces of art you could hang on your wall. They are so detailed they give you a good idea of how the film will look before it's even shot. You don't have to be an artist or go into that much detail to make your own story-boards. You just need to be able to get your ideas across.

I find it easier to sketch my storyboard first in pencil. When I'm happy with the layout and the structure of the shots, I then go over the pencil lines with a pen. People aren't easy to draw, and I'm no van Gogh, so I use a simple method: I draw an oval for the head and add just enough features to show expression. (Figure 16-1 shows storyboarded wide, mid, and close-up shots from a scene in our crew's film.)

If this is still a bit complicated, stick figures will do. You can then label your stick figures so you and your crew know which characters are being shown in the storyboard. (See Figure 16-2.) Labeling the character by the first letter of her name, or even just

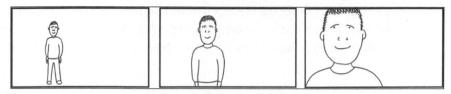

Figure 16-1

with A, B, and C is fine as long as you create a key or lookup table for people to use if they're not sure. The key or lookup table will have the letter followed by the name that it represents. In Figure 16-2, I created an example of a storyboard using labeled stick figures with a key to show the characters' names.

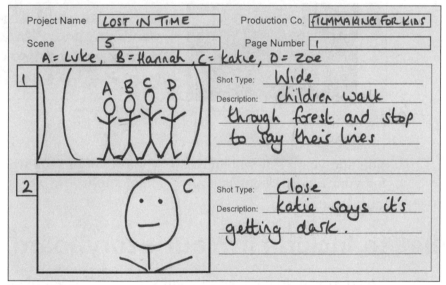

Figure 16-2

If drawing is not your thing, then you can always use photos for your storyboard. Get some friends to act as stand-ins for your actors, and then re-create the shots you want and photograph them with a still camera. You don't have to re-create the scene exactly or even use the location; the idea is just to show the types of shots you want to use. (Figure 16-3 shows an example of a photo storyboard our crew put together for a scene in their film.)

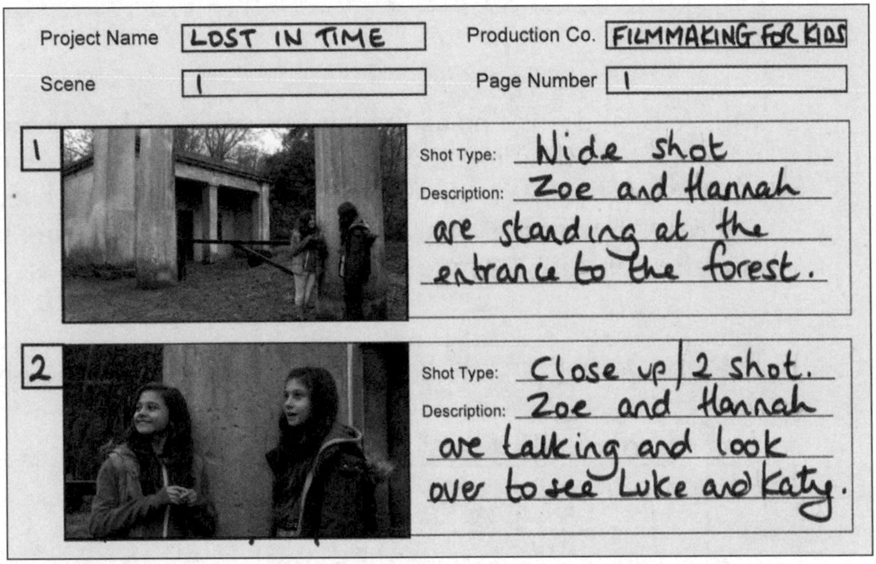

Project Name	LOST IN TIME	Production Co.	FILMMAKING FOR KIDS
Scene	1	Page Number	1

1 — Shot Type: Wide shot
Description: Zoe and Hannah are standing at the entrance to the forest.

2 — Shot Type: Close up / 2 shot.
Description: Zoe and Hannah are talking and look over to see Luke and Katy.

Figure 16-3

You and your crew will find a storyboard very useful when shooting your film. It also makes a nice memento from your first film.

What to Include in Your Storyboard

You may end up filming the scenes in your film out of order — you may want to shoot all the scenes in one location at one time or all nighttime scenes together. For this reason, creating separate storyboards for each scene is important so you can put your storyboards into the order they'll be filmed. A storyboard can also be used to make notes about a scene, including information about what the actors are wearing and details about props. This can be used as a reference when editing or shooting another scene to make sure that the actors are wearing the right clothes or the correct props are in place. Creating separate storyboards for each scene also means you can just take the storyboard you need for each scene when you go to your shooting location.

It's important to include information about the scenes on your storyboards so they don't get mixed up and you don't end up taking the wrong storyboard to the wrong shoot.

On you storyboard, be sure to include the following information:

- **Project name:** Include the name of your film or project. This can be a working title, which may not be the final title of the film. It's a provisional name you can use until you've decided. You may not decide on the final name of your film until the end of the production, during editing.

- **Production company:** Include the name of your production company or your name as the filmmaker. This means that if the storyboard is lost, whoever finds it may be able to return it to you.

- **Scene:** Include the scene number to allow you to sort the scene and match it to the scene script when filming.

- **Page number:** Include the page number because you may have more than one page and don't want to get the pages mixed up.

- **Shot number:** Include the shot number to show the order of the shots in your scene.

- **Shot image:** This is a drawing of what your shot will look like. Aim to show the shot type, the angle, and any expressions from your character.

- **Shot type:** Include your shot type so the camera operator knows how to frame the shot.

- **Description:** Write a brief description of the shot, including any special instructions to the crew or notes on the shot. You may want to include some of the dialogue to help match it to the script.

Try It Out Yourself

I created a blank storyboard for you to use, which can be down-loaded from this book's companion website.

Try storyboarding your film using the template I have created. Remember, you don't have to be an artist to make a storyboard, and this isn't a drawing competition. The aim is to show your crew how you'd like the shots to be framed and to make sure every shot on the storyboard is filmed and not omitted. Include information about the shot on your storyboard to help explain what you want your crew to capture.

After you've storyboarded your film, you can move on to the next project, where I show you how to enhance your shots using different angles and levels.

Enhancing Your Shots

In this project, I show you how to improve the look and feel of the shots you capture during filming by introducing different angles, levels, and styles. These can help make your film look great. I also share a camera-positioning technique that may keep you from distracting or confusing your audience.

There are many ways to enhance your shots. By simply changing the angle or raising or lowering the level of the camera, you can create dramatic-looking shots that transform your film. Enhancing your shots when filming helps capture the attention of your audience and can help build the emotion in a scene. It can also open up more options for the editor in post-production as there are different angles of the same scene to choose from.

One of the jobs of the director during filming is to look out for ways to enhance the shots using different angles and levels. You

often see directors walking round a set or location looking for the right angle or the best place to position the camera — looking, in other words, for ways to add impact and feeling into a shot.

My crew often laugh at me for this very reason. I'm always looking for ways to enhance shots, and I often want to film scenes again from new angles. They may laugh, but spending time getting those extra shots really pays off. It's better to have too much footage than not enough. You don't want to be left in the position of wishing that you'd taken the time to get more shots or another angle.

Viewing the Same Scene from Different Angles

One way of enhancing your film is to shoot a scene several times from different angles using different types of shots. For instance, you can film close-up shots, mid shots, and wide shots from different angles and cut them together when editing. This can make editing quite complicated, but the results look fantastic.

You can establish the setting for your scene with a wide shot, capture conversations with mid shots, and capture emotions and expressions with close-up shots. This helps keep your audience interested and will build emotions through the scene.

Figure 17-1 shows shots taken from the same moment in a scene but from different angles.

Figure 17-1

Filming a whole scene from different angles means that you can add the dialogue recorded in the close-up shots in your wide shots when editing. In the close-up shots, the microphone will be closer to the actor, so dialogue will be louder and clearer. For this to work well, however, the actors' lines must be delivered in the same way in each angle. This means your actors must keep to the script, so rehearsing is important.

Another way to enhance your shots when filming is to look at using objects in the foreground and background. Foreground is the areas between the actor or subject and the camera. Background is the area behind the subject or actor. Having objects in the foreground and background in a shot adds depth and makes the shot look more interesting. For example, if you're filming an actor walking through a park, you could place trees or park benches in the foreground or background.

Figure 17-2 shows a shot our crew took when filming. In the shot, a branch from a tree appears in the foreground as the actors walk in the background. This shot looks great and really enhances the look of the final film.

Figure 17-2

Adding Levels to Your Film

Filming from different angles and levels can affect the mood or feel of a shot. Filmmakers use levels all the time to help tell their story and to effect the way the audience should feel about a character.

Adding different levels to your scenes means changing the height of the camera in relation to your subject. For example, setting the camera lower than the subject to film from below or setting the camera higher than the subject to film from above.

There are many angles and levels to choose from. I explain some popular ones in the next few sections, and show why they are used within a scene.

Bird's-eye view

This angle involves filming from directly above your actors. (See Figure 17-3.) This is not easy to do unless you have access to a crane or a drone camera, or unless you film from a bridge.

Figure 17-3

Bird's-eye angles can look strange and are not often used in films, but when they are, they are normally used to show scale and the area of a scene. Using bird's-eye angles can make subjects look small and insignificant, like ants. They are often used in battle scenes to show the vast number of people in the battle or in desert scenes to show the vast open space around a character. I would avoid using bird's-eye angles unless you think it really enhances your film.

High-angle shot

This angle involves positioning the camera higher than the actors or subjects and looking down on them — although not from a vantage as high as the bird's-eye view. (See Figure 17-4.) To do this, you'll need a tripod that extends higher than your subjects or you may have to find a higher point to shoot from.

High-angle shots are often used in films to make the character or subject in the shot look weaker, more vulnerable, or less important. It can be used in a scene where the character should appear smaller than the other characters, such as if a character is being

Figure 17-4

bullied and you want to make him or her look less powerful. You can also use it in a scene where you want to show your character being scared or lost.

Eye-level shot

This angle involves the camera being placed at the level of the character's or subject's eye. (See Figure 17-5.) To achieve this, a tripod can be used, but if you're tall enough, you can hold the camera at eye level.

Eye-level shots are often used in films because they are *neutral,* which means they don't really suggest any particular meaning. For this reason, they are used in news reports and informational films. If you don't want to make your character look more or less important, or if you don't want to make a character look scared or scary, then eye-level is the angle to use.

Low-angle shot

This involves placing the camera lower than the subject or character, and looking up at them. (See Figure 17-6.) You can place the

Figure 17-5

Figure 17-6

camera on a tripod, or hold it in your hand, depending on your purposes. The camera should be lower than the subject. You could even rest the camera on the ground, pointing upwards, depending how dramatic you want your shot to look.

The low-angle shot is also known as the superhero shot because it can make a character look more powerful or more important to your audience. Aiming the camera up at your character makes your shot more dramatic. If you want a character to look more important or stronger than another character — such as when a character is bullying someone, an adult is talking to a child, or a superhero is saving someone — then the low-angle is the shot to use.

Point-of-view (POV) shots

This is where the camera acts as the character so the audience sees what the character sees. (See Figure 17-7.) To do this, you may want to ask your actor to hold the camera or simply ask your camera operator to move as the character would. Point-of-view shots are best filmed handheld because the movement adds realism to the shot.

Figure 17-7

Point-of-view shots are not used often, but when they are, they can add suspense and energy to the shot, such as in chase scenes to make the audience feel as if they are in the chase. They are also used in horror scenes to add suspense and make a scene more scary.

Dutch tilt

This is where the camera is purposely tilted to one side making the shot look off balance. (See Figure 17-8.) You can create this effect by simply tilting the camera to one side. If you are using a tripod you may have to lower one of the legs to create this effect.

The Dutch-tilt angle is also known as the *canted angle,* and it's used in a scene to make the shot look more dramatic and to purposely disturb the audience and make them feel uncomfortable. If you want to add a bit of madness to a character or make a scene feel uneasy, then the Dutch tilt is the angle to use. This technique should not be overused or used for no reason because it can distract your audience and could have the wrong effect on your scene.

Figure 17-8

Crossing the Line

As a filmmaker, the most important people to you are the audience — they're one of the reasons you make films. It's important to avoid upsetting or distracting your audience. One easy way to distract them is called *crossing the line* or *crossing the axis.* This happens when the audience's view of a scene changes so drastically that viewers end up distracted or confused. This may not sound like a big deal, but to a viewer, it's highly disorienting.

Some filmmakers choose to cross the line on purpose so as to add a sense of disorder or confusion to a scene. For example, you may cross the line in a fight or riot scene to add to the chaos and disorient the audience.

Figure 17-9 is a diagram showing a bird's-eye view of a scene in which two characters are having a conversation. I've drawn a line down the middle of the scene to show you how I have divided the scene and where I could place the cameras. My first camera angle is labeled "A" and note where I have placed my second camera labeled "B."

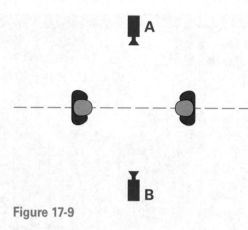

Figure 17-9

When editing, if I decide to cut from camera angle "A" to angle "B," it will look like my characters suddenly have swapped places. Figure 17-10 shows the footage from both camera angles; "A" and "B" show what the audience would see when changed from one to the other.

A   B

Figure 17-10

Crossing the line can confuse and disorient the audience. They may not even realize why they're confused, but they will notice something is wrong and may be distracted. Staying on one side of the line avoids confusion, and your shots will look great. This is called the *180-degree rule*. In Figure 17-11, I have labeled the positions where I could place my camera angles in this scene.

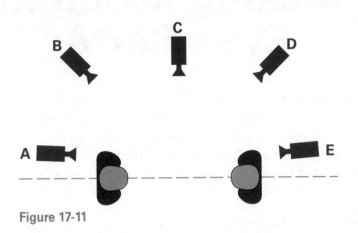

Figure 17-11

Camera angles "A" and "E" in Figure 17-11 are over-the-shoulder shots, and angle "C" is a mid shot showing both characters. Angles "B" and "D" could be used as mid shots to show both characters or as cut-in close-up shots to show hands or items on the table.

When you're setting up your scene, be sure to work out where your line is before you start filming. You don't need to draw an actual line, but just think about where your line is and avoid crossing it.

Try It Out Yourself

In this chapter, I show you ways to enhance your shots. Now it's time to look at the shots on your storyboard and work out how you can add feeling and emotion and to make them look interesting by using different camera angles and levels.

Making It Sound Even Better

Have you ever watched a video and struggled to hear the dialogue or noticed how bad the quality of the sound is? What is the point in writing dialogue for your actors to perform if your audience can't hear anything they're saying? This is why it's important to take the time to record the best and clearest sound when filming.

Sound is much harder to fix than video during the editing stage. Removing a noise that appears in the background of your dialogue is difficult to do without affecting the sound quality of that scene. Editing tools can help clean up the sound, but these only really make a small difference and can sometimes make it sound worse. The answer is to record the best quality sound when filming.

When filming, your sound operator needs to be constantly listening out for unwanted noises or sound issues. You need to make sure your sound operator knows that if he or she hears any unwanted sound, he or she needs to shout "cut" to stop filming. It's pointless to continue filming if there is a problem with the sound. When the sound is clear again, the shot can be taken again.

In Project 3, I discuss how important sound is to your film and how to record great sound. In this project, I show you how to record even better sound when filming.

Microphone Techniques for Dialogue

The key to recording dialogue is placing the microphone as close as possible to your actor without the microphone appearing in the shot. Also, aiming the microphone in the direction of the sound helps to keep the dialogue clear. (See Figure 18-1.)

Figure 18-1

If you're using an external microphone on a boom pole or a hand-held, it's important to keep it as still as possible when recording because this prevents the device from picking up any noises from the boom operator. Microphones are very sensitive and can pick up noises, including from the hands holding them.

The best way to detect unwanted noises is through a pair of headphones. Without headphones, any unwanted noise can easily go undetected, noticed only when you're importing the footage into the editing tool later. The headphones you see being worn in the image at the beginning of this chapter are called *closed-back* headphones, which surround the ears and cut out most of the noise coming from the outside, so that the person monitoring sound can mainly hear what is being picked up by the microphone. These can be expensive, but a budget pair starts at only around $10.

If you hear a distracting background noise through the headphones when filming, such as from a plane, gust of wind, or passing car, stop filming and wait for the sound to pass, and then retake that shot. If the sound of a plane appears in the background in one shot and not in the next, the sound will be uneven between shots, and this will sound odd for your audience.

The following list describes a few ways to avoid recording unwanted noises during filming:

- Turn off any air-conditioning units or fan heaters while filming. Microphones can pick up noises that sometimes we can't even hear when filming.

- Make sure all cellphones are off or on silent when filming because if they go off, they can bring a shoot to a stop. Also, sometimes a cellphone's roaming or searching signal can interfere with the camera and can be heard on the recorded audio.

- Avoid pointing the microphone in the direction of any clear background noise, including roads, waterfalls, or fountains. Again, these sounds can come across clearly in the recording and can make it hard to hear dialogue.

- Avoid filming in empty rooms because they can create distracting echoes in your recording (unless, of course, you *want* echoes in your film). To eliminate echoes, place hand blankets on walls to help deaden the sound.

Dealing with Wind

Sound operators often have wind problems when filming outside. Not *that* kind of wind — the sky kind of wind!

When filming outside, you may pick up noise from the wind through the microphone, which can sometimes make your actors' dialogue hard to hear. The noise is caused by the wind hitting the microphone. If you're not sure what this sounds like, try gently blowing on the microphone on your camera and listen through the headphones — it's not a nice sound at all.

Wind noise can really only be detected by monitoring the sound using headphones during filming.

If you can hear wind noise when filming, then you need a windshield or a dead cat. (Not a *real* dead cat; it's just another name for a windshield.) A *windshield* is a furry cover placed over the microphone to protect it from the wind. Windshields are also available for onboard microphones on video cameras.

Figure 18-2 shows an example of two types of windshield available for external microphones. (Now you can see why they're sometimes called "dead cats.")

Figure 18-2

Figure 18-3 shows what both microphones look like without the windshields.

Figure 18-3

If you still have wind noise when filming, try booming from under-neath or forming a barrier between the wind and the microphone to shelter the microphone from wind noise.

Checking Levels as You Record

Most camcorders now have audio meters that allow you to see how loud or how soft the sound being recorded is. The audio meters usually appear on the LCD monitor on your camcorder. You can use these meters to check the levels of the sound before filming and to make sure that the sound you're recording isn't so loud it will distort or isn't so quiet the audience won't be able to hear the dialogue. Some camcorders allow you to change the levels of your microphone manually, but others do this automatically. Either way, make sure you check the audio levels before and during filming.

Figure 18-4 shows you what the audio meter looks like on the camera our crew used.

When checking the audio levels before filming, ask your actors to say some of their lines at the volume they would perform them when filming. You'll be able to see from the audio meters how high the levels are, and these can be adjusted if the audio is too loud or too quiet. The bars should not be constantly *peaking*, which means hitting the end of the meter, which is usually red. (See Figure 18-5.) If a meter does this, then the audio levels are too loud.

Figure 18-4

Figure 18-5

If the audio levels are too quiet, on the other hand, then the audio meter bars won't rise as much. (See Figure 18-6.)

Figure 18-6

Don't worry if your camera doesn't have any audio-level meters. In that case, you can always listen to see whether the audio is too loud or too quiet. By plugging headphones into your camera and listening to the dialogue, you'll be able to hear if the audio is too loud, because it will distort and be uncomfortable to listen to. On the other hand, if you can hardly hear what your actor is saying, then you either need to turn the microphone volume up, move the microphone closer to your actor, or ask him or her to speak louder.

It's a good idea to ask a crew member to check the audio levels during filming. An assigned crew member can concentrate on watching and listening to the sound levels while the director concentrates on the shots and the actors' performances. The person monitoring the audio can look at the audio level meter and listen through the headphones for any noises that may distract your audience.

Try It Out Yourself

You now know how to record even better sound, so why not give it a go? Before you move on to the next project, record some sound through your onboard or external microphone. Record some dialogue, check for wind noises, and check the level as you record to make sure it's not too quiet or too loud.

In the next project, I show you how to use light (or a lack of it) to add mood to your shots.

Adding Mood with Lighting

Using lighting in film can be very effective and help to create feelings and emotions in your audience, but using darkness can be just as effective. It's important for the audience to be able to see your subjects or characters, but using a mixture of light and dark can really enhance your shots.

It's amazing what lighting can do to a shot. By simply moving a light or using shadows, you can change the mood of your footage. Lighting designers and gaffers spend years learning about light and how it can be used in film, and when you light your scenes, you'll see why. Next time you watch a film, have a look at how the shots are lit. See if you can work out how they created an effect or a look in a scene.

In this project, I show you how to use lighting effects to add mood and to make your shots look great.

Using lights when filming can create reflections in windows and shiny surfaces. When you set up your shot, check the viewfinder on your camera for reflections from the lights. You can be avoid these by moving the light, repositioning the camera, or avoiding filming towards windows and shiny surfaces.

Using Shadows and Lighting Effects

There are so many ways your can use light and shadows to create a mood in a shot. You don't always need to light every area of a scene or actor.

If you're looking to create a more scary or creepy feel to your shots, use a shadow effect: When filming in a dark room, for example, you can cast a shadow over one side of an actor's face by simply placing a light to one side of him or her. Figure 19-1 shows how this looks.

Figure 19-1

This effect is often used in films because it can create a darker mood and make your character look more scary.

If you want to create an outline around your character so as not to see the features on his or her face, place the light behind and slightly to one side of your actor. This creates a white outline that shows a character without revealing who he or she is. This can be used to build suspense. Figure 19-2 shows how this looks.

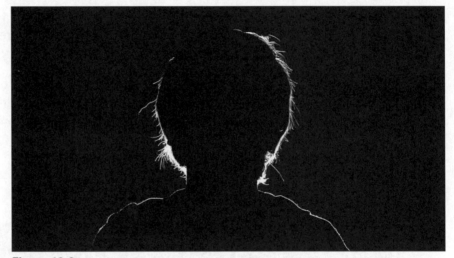

Figure 19-2

Another way to create mood and feeling in a shot is to use a character's own shadows. You can do this by placing a light to one side of the camera that shines on to the actor. This can make your shot look more scary or add suspense, if needed. Figure 19-3 shows what this looks like.

The lower the height of the light, the taller the shadow will be. You may also just want to film the shadow and not the character, which can be used to make a scene look even more scary and creepy.

Another way to add a scary or creepy feel to your film is to simply film the shadows your subjects make on the floor.

Figure 19-3

Using Colored Gels and Filters

There are different colors of light, which is measured in kelvin. This determines how cold or how warm the color of light is. Daylight is in the middle of the scale. If your shot is cold or too blue in color, then you can set your camera's white balance higher to make the shot look warmer and more natural. If you're shooting indoors using the lights in your house, your shots may look orange or red, and lowering the white balance setting on your camera will make your shot look more natural. Most cameras have an automatic white balance setting, which measures the color of the light in the room and changes the white balance setting automatically. I always like to set my white balance manually, however, because sometimes the camera gets it wrong. To find out how to adjust the white balance on your camera, have a look at the camera's instructions.

You can get different types of filters for film lights that can change the color and mood of a shot. These filter gels are specifically designed for use with studio lights, so they can withstand high temperatures. Some homemade options may not cope with high temperatures as well and could be a fire risk. Colored filter gel sheets can be bought from camera stores (such as www.bhphotovideo.com) for around $5 per sheet, or you can save money by buying them in variety packs. Some lights come with colored filters, as shown in Figure 19-4.

Figure 19-4

If you want to create a moonlight effect for a nighttime shot, for example, you can use a blue filter or you could lower the white balance on your camera to create a more blue and cold feel. If you want to create a warmer more sunny effect, on the other hand, you could use an orange or yellow filter over your light or increase the white balance setting on your camera.

Figure 19-5 shows shots of our actor with and without a blue filter. The blue filter throws a blue light that makes the shot look cold.

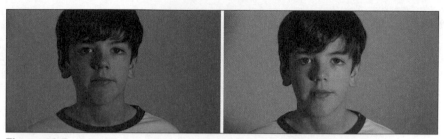

Figure 19-5

Most lights used for film can be quite harsh and can create strong shadows around the subject or character. To reduce these shadows, use diffusion filter paper (also called a *scrim*), which, when placed over your lights, spreads the light over a scene. This helps reduce shadows and create a more natural-looking light. It also softens the light on your actors' skin. Figure 19-6 shows a shot of our actor with and without diffusion paper. Diffusion paper designed for studio lights can be bought from camera stores for around $5 per sheet.

Light doesn't always have to be used on a subject. You can use lights to light the background of a scene instead, which adds depth to a shot. You could also add a colored gel to the background light to throw some color on the background.

Any light you add to a scene needs to have a reason. For example, adding a blue filtered light onto one side of an actor's face would look odd to viewers unless there was a good reason for it to be there — such as, say, to represent the moonlight shining through the window onto the actor.

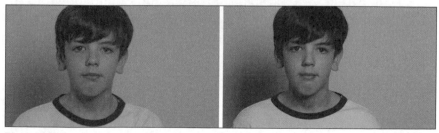

Figure 19-6

Getting the Best from Daylight

If you're filming outside, you're limited to the available daylight, which of course changes throughout the year. In summer, daylight lasts longer during the day, so you can film earlier in the morning until later at night. This is a good thing — early in the morning tends to be a good time to shoot if you don't want to be interrupted by the public. I aim to shoot outside scenes as early as possible because there are fewer people about and because the light looks great when the sun is lower in the sky. Many big-budget films are shot during the summer months because of the longer hours of daylight. Winter months tend to have a shorter number of hours of daylight, although this depends on where you are in the world; the sun rises and sets at different times at different times of the year.

Twice a day, once in the morning and once in the evening, the sun is low in the sky and produces perfect light for filming. Filmmakers call these periods the *golden hour* or the *magic hour*. This is usually 45 minutes to an hour after sunrise and 45 minutes to an hour before sunset. The time varies depending on the time of year and the part of the world in which you live. During the golden hour, the low sun makes light appear soft and warm or more yellow in color. It's a lovely time to film because the sun casts long shadows and your shots can look magical.

If you're not sure what time the golden hour is where you live, you can check online to see what time sunrise and sunset are. You can also get apps to tell you what time the golden hour is. The app I use is from the Apple App Store and is called Magic Hour. It's great — it uses your location and counts down to the next golden hour on that day. It also tells you what time the next golden hour begins and ends.

Try It Out Yourself

Before you move on to the next project, practice adding mood to a shot using light. Cast shadows on the face of your subject, cast shadows of your subjects onto the wall behind them, and use colored filters to add color effects to a scene.

In the next project, I show you how to direct your actors and crew, and how to log your shots when shooting your short film.

Time to Film

Now it's time to shoot your short film. In this project, all the hard work you put into planning and preparing your film pays off. I love this part of the filmmaking process because it's where the story and the characters come alive.

By this point, you will have rehearsed with your actors to develop their characters and to make sure they know their lines. You will have also met with your team to talk through the scenes and explain the shots using your storyboard so they will know what to expect on filming days. All of this saves time and makes your cast and crew feel more comfortable on the day of filming.

In this project, I show you how to start shooting your short film so that it's ready to edit together later.

Directing Your Film

As a director, you're responsible for getting the best from your crew and actors in the time available to you. It's important, then, to keep track of time. During filming, time goes very quickly, and you could easily end up rushing things at the end of the shoot in order to fit everything in. In fact, this is a pretty common problem. I've been on many film shoots that started out calm and relaxed and ended up tense and frantic as the filmmakers struggled to complete the shot list for that day. I've also made the mistake of thinking that someone else was watching the time and only later found out that no one was. Accordingly, a wristwatch is a useful tool to have on hand so you can quickly check the time without disturbing a scene or the actors during their performance.

Keep concerns about time in mind even before the shoot, when you're planning your filming day. Try not to plan too much filming into one day. Actors and crew get tired at the end of a long day, and their performance will suffer.

Filmmaking: An easy job?

People often think that filmmaking is an easy job, but the truth is that it's often hard work. It can be fun, but it can take long days, and it can be tiring. As a filmmaker, you're doing many things at once, especially if you have a small crew, and you're on your feet all day, walking around, concentrating on the performance of your actors and the tasks your crew are doing. It can also be quite stressful, especially if something goes wrong or if you're struggling with time or with the weather. So never let anyone tell you that it's all easy!

Filmmaking can be fun, and that's a good thing, but you have to be careful. Playing around on the set can easily end up wasting the time available for your day's shoot. When an actor messes up a line or a scene goes unexpectedly wrong, everyone may laugh and be distracted. This is fine, of course, but you must do what you can to refocus the crew and cast as quickly as possible. In fact, this may be one of your primary jobs as a director. Being the kill-joy isn't always the easiest or most popular thing to do, but no one else is likely to do it. An actor or crew member may get the giggles after a mistake and may struggle to focus again. When this happens, you may have to call a five-minute break to allow him or her time to get over it. On my film shoots, this has happened many times, sometimes leaving us no choice but to cut some important shots from a scene, and affecting the final film.

When filming scenes with dialogue between two or more people, remember to film reaction shots from each actor when other actors are talking. These reaction shots can be great to use to show responses and emotions and to cover up any issues with other shots if needed when editing. You can record these reaction shots when you film the actor's close-up shot. I sometimes record an extra shot of just reactions from an actor. To do this, I talk the actor through the reactions I want while filming. (The audio for these reaction shots can be taken out when editing.)

Before filming, make sure all members of the cast and crew on set have turned off their cellphones or switched them onto airplane mode because cameras can sometimes pick up interference noises from cellphones as they ring or search network signal.

When you start filming, remember to take your script and story-boards along with you. You can use them to make sure that you get all the shots you planned and that you can prompt the actors, if needed.

Logging Your Shots

During a film shoot, you'll be capturing a lot of footage. Because your actors made some mistakes or because you wanted to take a few extra shots for safety, you may end up with several versions of the same angle or shot. During editing, these shots will look similar, which makes it hard to know which shot was the one you liked the best. For this reason, I always make notes about each shot captured on a shot log sheet, which makes editing much easier and ensures you don't miss the best take from each angle.

A shot log can be completed by an assistant director or by the director if you have a small crew. Ideally, the shot log will be the sole responsibility of one person during the shoot. I've been involved in film shoots that didn't use a shot log sheet, which made editing very difficult, especially if you don't edit the film straightaway, because you're likely to forget which shots were the best.

Some shot log sheets can get very complicated, especially for big-budget films, because they record information about the footage, including details of timecode, type of lens, focus, and filters, which isn't always needed for smaller productions. The following list includes useful information for you to note on your shot log sheet when filming:

✔ **Shoot date:** This is simply the date that you're filming the shots you log into your shot log sheet. This can be very useful when importing your footage and editing because it helps to track your footage and refer back to your shot log sheet at a later date.

✔ **Page number:** Here you enter the page number for the shot log sheet you're completing. You may find that you end up working with more than one sheet, so it's important to number the pages. That way you can keep the shots in the order they were filmed.

✔ **Project name:** Here's where you complete the name of the film — a working title or a final title — you are shooting. This is very useful for me because I'm always working on multiple projects at once. Including the name helps me make sure I don't get my shot log sheets mixed up with others I'm working on at the same time.

✔ **Production company:** Enter the name of your production company or the name of the director here. This can be useful if your shot log sheets go missing because if they're found, the finder may be able to send them back to you.

✔ **Clip number or name:** This is where you enter the name of the clip or the number of the clip on the media card you're recording to. (By "clip," here, I mean a segment of video recorded as a file to the media card or tape.) Some cameras will show the name of the clip when you watch the footage back on the camera. If your camera doesn't show the clip name, just enter the clip number, which will be "1" for your first shot. I normally record a few seconds of nothing at the beginning of a shoot so I can find out what the clip name is and make sure that the camera is working okay. I record this first clip on the shot log sheet as "test shot" so that the shot information doesn't get mixed up, confusing me when editing.

✔ **Scene number:** This is where you enter the scene number that you're filming. This is useful because you may end up shooting more than one scene in a day, and because you may end up filming your scenes out of order. By recording the scene number, your shot log sheet will help you organize your clips when importing and editing your footage.

✔ **Take number:** Here you enter the number of times a shot has been taken. (The number of "takes.") This number resets every time you change the angle or shot. If you set up a close-up, for instance, the first recording you make from this angle gives you the take number of 1. If you retake this shot without changing the angle, the take number will then be 2. Tracking takes helps you keep track of the number of times you filmed a shot. Usually, of course, the last take is the best.

✔ **Shot description:** This is where you enter the details about the shot you're filming. Here you may wish to note information about the shot type, the characters in the frame, and what happens in the shot. This information helps you identify the shot when importing and editing the footage.

✔ **Comments:** Here you can enter any notes about the shot and how it went while filming. Include information about any mistakes made, reasons for retaking the shot, or if it was a good take or not. Here you can also make notes about which was the best take. This is the most useful part of the shot log sheet when importing and editing your footage because these notes can help you decide whether to use the shot in the final edit or not.

Figure 20-1 shows an example of the shot log sheet used by our crew on their short film. You can also download a sample shot log sheet from the website.

SHOOT DATE: 01 / 10 / 2014				PAGE NUMBER: 1
PROJECT NAME: Lost in Time				PRODUCTION CO: Filmmaking for Kids

CLIP NO. / NAME	SCENE NO.	TAKE NO.	SHOT DESCRIPTION	COMMENTS
AA4523			Test shot	
AA4524	1	1	Wide shot / tilt down	Cut too early - retake
AA4525	1	2	Wide shot / tilt down	Mistake - retake
AA4526	1	3	Wide shot / tilt down	Good take
AA4527	1	1	Close on Hannah	Good take
AA4528	1	1	Close on Zoe	Good take
AA4529	1	1	Mid shot on all actors	Cropped actors head - retake
AA4530	1	2	Mid shot on all actors	Good take
AA4531	2	1	Wide - enter forest	Mistake - retake
AA4532	2	2	Wide - enter forest	Good take
AA4533	2	1	Close - Feet walking	Good take
AA4534	2	1	POV - trees	Water on lens - retake
AA4535	2	2	POV - trees	Shakey cam - retake

Figure 20-1

Checking Your Shots

When filming, it's hard to really know what your footage looks like until you import it onto your computer and watch it. Watching the scene through the small viewfinder on your camcorder can make it difficult to tell whether your subject is in focus or if any of the shots are too dark or too bright. Sometimes sunlight can make it even harder. This is why it's important to check your clips as often as possible during your shoot. I like to view the video clips back on my laptop or through a monitor to check that the footage is okay to use. By doing this, I usually spot mistakes from the crew or actors or if something is in the shot that shouldn't be. When checking the shots, you may also notice any issues with the audio, such as wind noise. When filming, you're so busy concentrating on the many different things to look out for that you can't pay all of your attention to any one thing, so it's easy to miss errors. Even if you don't have a laptop or monitor, watching the footage back through the camera is better than not doing it at all. By checking your clips often during your shoot, you can reshoot a scene or shot without disrupting your filming schedule too much. On the other hand, if you wait to check your shots during the edit, the mistakes you find may force you to call your actors and crew back to reshoot the scene on another day.

Another thing I like to do between filming scenes is to edit some of the captured footage. If I don't get a chance to edit between scenes, at the end of a day's shoot, I often download the clips to my computer. I'll look through the footage, and sometimes I'll place some of the clips into a timeline and assemble a rough edit of the scenes filmed during that day. This is only a simple, quick version of the edit, of course, because I'll spend far more time on editing at the end of the process, when all filming is complete. Editing between scenes allows me to see how the shots look, to ensure the story is being told through the captured footage, and to make note of anything I may need to add to help tell the story. It can also make the editing process simpler: It can be easier to choose the best shots at that stage — because you filmed those shots earlier that day, the best shots are still fresh in your mind. This helps reduce editing time later, since the selected clips will already be in the timeline.

Try It Out Yourself

Are you ready to film your short film? It's time to call your actors and crew and start filming your first short film. Remember to use your script, storyboard, shot list, and shot log sheet to keep track of what needs to be filmed and what has been filmed.

In the next project, I show you how to get the "film look" and how to enhance the sound when editing your short film.

Getting the Film Look with Editing

Now it's time to bring the footage you've captured together to build your film in the timeline in your editing tool. I will be using iMovie to edit the short film in this project.

It's amazing what you can do in the editing tool to make your shots look more cinematic and professional. Modern editing technology can do wonders. Keep in mind, though, that this doesn't diminish the importance of filming great shots. It's important to spend time making your shots look good when filming — the editing process only makes them look better.

Editors working on large-scale films spend months changing the color and look of each shot in the editing tool. That way, each shot has the same look and feel, and all the shots flow together perfectly. Don't worry, however, you won't need to spend that much time editing your film — unless, of course, you want to. Spending more time on the edit of your film helps improve the quality of the final result.

Professional editors use very expensive and complicated editing tools to enhance the shots in the films they work on, but it's still possible to improve your footage using the basic editing tools on a Mac and PC. In this project, I show you how to enhance the look and sound of your footage in the editing tool to make your film look great.

Editing Angles and Shots Together

Project 17 discussed the different angles and shots you can use when filming and how these can improve the look and feel of your film. Using these different angles and shots can keep your audience interested and help build emotions within a scene.

Here's where you start pasting all those shots together. To get started, follow these steps:

1. **Open iMovie and create a new event in which to place your footage. Name the event with the title of your film.**

2. **Import your film footage into the new event.**

   To be reminded about how to import footage in to your event, revisit Project 5.

3. **Within your new event, create a new movie project with no theme. Name the project with the title of your film.**

   After all your footage has been imported, you can edit the different angles together in the timeline.

4. **Decide which shot you want your first scene to start with —
   this will be your establishing shot. Select the footage from the event that you want to use as the first shot or the establishing shot. Drag this footage into the timeline.**

   Remember to select the area of the clip you want to include before dragging it into the timeline. This cuts out any unwanted footage before or after the selected area.

In our crew's film, their establishing shot was a wide shot of the scene with a tilt down from the sky to the character at the beginning. Their first scene starts with two characters, Hannah and Zoe, having a conversation, but the dialogue will not be heard as it's not important to the story. At this point, music plays to cover the dialogue.

5. **Think carefully about which clip you want to use as your second shot. Select your second clip and drag it into the timeline after the first clip, as shown in Figure 21-1.**

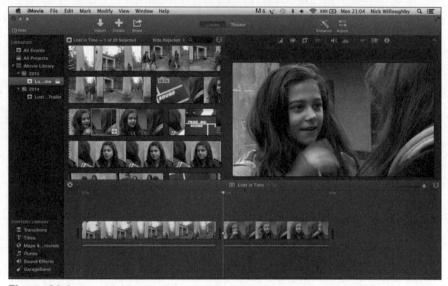

Figure 21-1

Watch the two clips together and see how they flow from one to the other in the timeline. You may wish to adjust the end point of the first clip or start point of the second clip to make the transition smoother between the two shots.

Remember, you can make the clip longer or shorter by selecting the clip and hovering over the beginning or end of the clip until you see two arrows pointing away from each other, and then dragging to the left or right.

In our crew's wide shot in their first scene, Hannah brings her hand up to move her hair out of her face. In Hannah's close-up, she does the same thing. This will look great if we can cut together the wide shot and the close-up at the point when she lifts her hand. Figure 21-2 shows the wide shot and close-up shot cut together at this moment.

Figure 21-2

6. **Choose a third clip to follow the second clip in your timeline. Select the area of footage that you want to use as the third shot and drag it into the timeline after the second shot, as shown in Figure 21-3.**

Figure 21-3

Our crew decided to cut to a close-up of Zoe as their third shot.

7. **Select the footage you want to use as the fourth shot and drag it after the third shot in the timeline, as shown in Figure 21-4.**

Figure 21-4

Our film crew used the wide angle shot again as their fourth clip. In this shot, two new characters, Katie and Luke, walk into the scene.

8. **Select the footage you want to use as the fifth shot and drag it after the fourth shot in the timeline, as shown in Figure 21-5.**

For the last shot in their first scene, our crew used a mid shot of the characters as they discuss entering the forest.

Keep adding footage until your scene is complete. Scene 1 is now edited using the different types of shots and angles captured when filming. You can now move on to editing the following scenes using the same steps.

Figure 21-5

Editing Dialogue and Inserting Reaction Shots

I'm now going to show you how to edit different angles and shots with dialogue together in the timeline. To demonstrate this, I'm moving forward to scene 7 in our crew's film. In this scene, there are quite a lot of angles to edit together.

At the beginning of scene 7, a character, Luke, stops the others in the forest and tells them they are in danger. Because the character is very weak, at some point he falls to the ground. He falls out of frame in a mid over-the-shoulder shot and the other characters crowd round him. To continue the dialogue and conversation from here, we need to change the angle and use the close-ups and mid shots for the dialogue from each actor. In the edit, we changed the angle as Luke fell to make the transition look as natural and smooth as possible. Figure 21-6 shows the cut point between these angles.

Figure 21-6

From the new angle, Luke now delivers a few lines of dialogue. As he talks, our crew decided to add a reaction shot from a character in the group surrounding him to show a response to what Luke is saying. You can place this extra shot over the main clip in your timeline as an overlay clip by following these steps:

1. **Decide which footage you want to place over your the main clip in your timeline.**

2. **Click on the selected footage, and then hold and drag it into the timeline above the clip you want to place this footage over, as shown in Figure 21-7.**

Figure 21-7

Now that your overlay clip is above the main clip in the timeline, you will want to mute the sound in the overlay clip because it may not be needed. In the overlay clip we placed in our timeline, there are sounds of people talking and cars going past, and none of this is wanted.

To mute the sound in this overlay clip, follow these steps:

1. **Select the overlay clip in the timeline and hover over the volume adjustment bar within the clip, as shown in Figure 21-8.**

Adjust volume

Figure 21-8

2. **Click, hold, and drag this bar to the bottom of the overlay clip, as shown in Figure 21-9.**

   This overlay clip is now muted. All you should be able to hear when playing the footage back is the sound from the main clip.

Figure 21-9

When Luke finishes talking, Hannah has a line, so we need to cut to the appropriate shot of her. When a character says a line, it's best to show the character speaking on-screen (often in a close-up shot) so the audience knows who's talking. However, this is not always important, and even when it is, it doesn't always have to be a close-up shot. In the case of our crew's film, however, Hannah does say her line in a close-up shot, so we must cut to this after Luke has finished saying his line. To add the next angle into the timeline, follow these steps:

1. **Choose the footage you want to add to the timeline.**

2. **Click, hold, and drag the selected footage into the timeline after the last shot, as shown in Figure 21-10.**

You don't want to hold on a shot longer than needed before you bring in the next angle. You can trim the beginning and end of your clips to take away any unwanted footage. This makes your transitions look more natural and smooth. Be careful not to cut any of your dialogue off when trimming your footage. You can see where the dialogue is in the timeline by looking at the bottom of the clips. An audio waveform, which

Figure 21-10

looks like a mountain range, appears there as well, as shown in Figure 21-11. This shows where sound appears, most likely when someone is talking.

Audio waveform

Figure 21-11

Creating the Film Look with Color and Effects

After all the shots have been placed into the timeline and cut together, the next step is to color-correct and grade the footage in the timeline. Color-correcting and grading, which involves enhancing the look of the clips to add mood and atmosphere, is a process usually done only after all the clips have been added to the timeline. There are many ways to color-correct and grade your film, and in this section I show you a few of them. Some editors prefer to add a colored filter, whereas others prefer to change the amount of color saturation. iMovie has some great filters and effects, but other editing tools offer more advanced features.

Making color corrections

Because our crew's film is a thriller, they wanted to add a dark, scary look to their shots. You may want to add a different feel and look to yours. Either way, you can view and add the effects to your footage by following the steps below. First, click the Adjust button above the preview window to make sure the adjustments bar appears, as shown in Figure 21-12. Then you can make color corrections to your clips by following these steps:

1. **Select the clip in the timeline that you wish to adjust.**

2. **Click on the color correction button in the adjustment bar to show the options available, as shown in Figure 21-13.**

   For the clip in the preview window, our crew decided to increase the highlights by a very small amount and drop the shadows to give more depth to the shot. This can add a more cinematic look to your shots. Steps 3 through 5 show you how.

3. **Make sure the clip you want to adjust is selected in the timeline.**

4. **Click and hold the highlight slider, which is marked by a yellow circle in Figure 21-14, and drag it to the right or left to increase or decrease the lighter areas in your shot.**

Figure 21-12

Figure 21-13

5. Click and hold the Shadows slider, which is marked by a red circle in Figure 21-14, and drag it to the right or left to increase or decrease the darker areas of your shot.

Figure 21-14

Figure 21-15 shows a still frame from the clip I adjusted before and after increasing the lighter areas and decreasing the darker areas in the shot.

Before adjusting lighter/
darker areas

After adjusting lighter/
darker areas

Figure 21-15

Adjusting color saturation

The next adjustment our crew made to their shot was to decrease the color saturation slightly. This takes away the color in the video and adds a more cinematic look and feel to your shot.
To do this, follow these steps:

1. **Make sure the clip you want to adjust is selected in the timeline.**

2. **Click and hold the Saturation slider, which is marked by a red circle in Figure 21-16, and drag it left or right to decrease or increase the color saturation in the shot.**

Figure 21-17 shows a still frame from the clip I adjusted before and after decreasing the saturation in the shot.

Figure 21-16

Before saturation   After saturation

Figure 21-17

Changing color temperature

The last color correction adjustment our crew wanted to do was to lower the color temperature to make the shot look colder, as though it were shot near nightfall. By this point in the film, the sky should be getting dark but this scene was filmed during the day. To correct this, we can lower the color temperature to make it look like the sky is getting dark. If you wanted to add a more warm look to your film, on the other hand — that is, to make the sun appear to be shining — you can simply increase the color temperature. You can change your color temperature by following these steps:

1. **Make sure the clip you want to adjust is selected in the timeline.**

2. **Click and hold the Color temperature slider, which is marked by the red circle in Figure 21-18, and drag left or right to make the shot look cooler or warmer.**

Figure 21-18

Adding effects

Let's have a look at the effects that can be added to your shots. To add effects to your clips, follow these steps:

1. **Make sure the clip to which you want to add the effect is selected in the timeline.**

2. **Click on the Video and Audio Effects button in the adjustments bar, as shown in Figure 21-19.**

Figure 21-19

3. **To see the list of available video effects, click the None button, as shown in Figure 21-20.**

4. **Hover over the effects to preview how they look with your clip.**

5. **Click on the effect you want to use to apply it to the selected clip.**

Figure 21-20

Our crew chose to use the Vignette effect on their clips because it adds depth to the shot and focuses the attention on the characters. It darkens the edges of the clip, which also helps to make it look like the sky is getting dark. Figure 21-21 compares the finished clip to the original version.

Now you can color-correct and add effects to the rest of the clips in your timeline to make your shots look amazing.

Original   With Vignette effect

Figure 21-21

Enhancing the Sound

Good sound is hard to record, and it's not always easy to repair or fix when editing. This is why it's important to have someone listening and monitoring the sound throughout filming. When importing and reviewing your footage, you may find you need to make some clips louder because the recording levels were too low when filming. You can see this from the audio waveform in the clip: If the sound levels are too low, the peaks in the mountain-shaped pattern will not be very tall. The closer to the volume adjustment bar the peaks are, the higher the louder the sound levels are. In Figure 21-22, the sound in the clip highlighted in red is lower than the sound highlighted in yellow because the audio waveforms are at different heights.

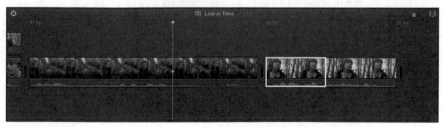

Figure 21-22

You can make changes to the sound levels when editing by following these steps:

1. **Select the clip to which you wish to make changes.**

2. **Hover over the volume adjustment bar until two arrows pointing away from each other appear. Drag the bar up to increase the sound volume or down to decrease the sound volume, as shown in Figure 21-23.**

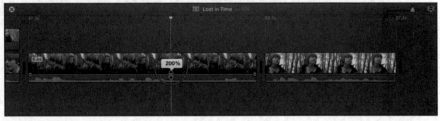

Figure 21-23

The location our crew found to shoot their short film was near a road so the sound of cars passing in the background appears throughout the footage. It is possible to reduce constant background noises when editing, but usually it takes some expensive and complicated software to do it. However, iMovie has a built-in noise reduction feature. It's not the best tool on the market, but it can help you reduce the background noise in your film. To use this feature, follow these steps:

1. **Select the clip to which you want to make changes.**

2. **Click the Noise Reducer and Equalizer button in the adjustments bar, as shown in Figure 21-24.**

3. **Click the Reduce Background Noise check box, as shown in Figure 21-25.**

4. **Change the level of the Noise Reduction slider depending on how much is needed.**

Setting the Noise Reduction slider too high can make the audio or dialogue sound unnatural and muddy. Too much noise reduction can make actors sound like they are underwater. Most of the time, only a small amount of noise reduction is needed to improve the quality of the audio.

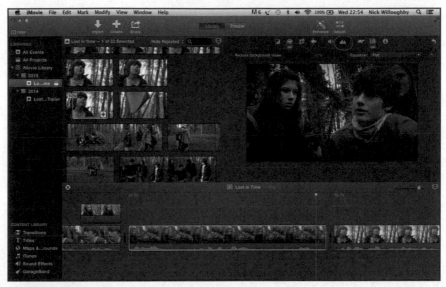

Figure 21-24

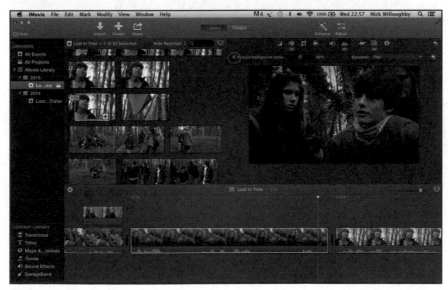

Figure 21-25

Try It Out Yourself

You can now add the audio effects to the rest of your clips, add any music that you would like to help build the emotions within your scenes, add titles at the beginning and credits at the end, and finally have your film ready to show your family and friends.

In the next project, I show you how to get reviews and comments on your film and use them to develop and improve your skills as a filmmaker.

Getting a Film Review

Wow, can you believe it? You're at the last project in this book. You've done it! You've created your first short film — well done! Now it's time to look back at what you've done and review your work.

So, why do we make films? Is it for our own enjoyment? Is it to entertain other people? Ideally, it's a mixture of both. Most filmmakers get their enjoyment from making films that their audience enjoys watching.

Good filmmakers are always searching — they're searching for new ideas for stories, for new approaches or filming styles, and most of all, for ways to improve what they do. The best way to improve and develop your skills as a filmmaker is to keep creating ideas, keep making films, and keep reviewing your work.

After making a film, I often get quite nervous about showing the film to other people. It's only natural, really. I worry about what they might think, even as I realize how important it is to get feedback from them. Getting feedback from your audience helps shape what you do in the future with your next films.

In this project, I show you how to review your film, how to get feedback from other people, and how to use the feedback to grow and develop as a filmmaker.

Reviewing Your Work

Has anyone ever told you "you are your own worst critic"? This means that sometimes you spot mistakes or problems with your work that others wouldn't notice. Seeing these otherwise-invisible flaws is a common ailment in the creative arts. In fact, you may find your finished film hard to watch because you'll notice all those mistakes or things you could have done better. This is fine, but try not to be too hard on yourself or too negative about your work when you do notice mistakes. Keep in mind that you'll only get better as a filmmaker. Some of my first films are full of mistakes and problems, but I can now look back and see how much I've improved since then. At the time, I found it hard to watch my films because I noticed so many problems. I could have easily given up, but I learned from my mistakes and used what I learned to create my next films.

After you have made your film, it's important to write down the things you learned through making it and the things you want to change the next time you make a film. The sooner after making your film that you do this, the better. By moving quickly, the

process will still be fresh in your mind. Then you can start applying these changes to your next film. Before reviewing my films,
I like to export them from the editing tool so I can watch them
back on the media player on my computer or sometimes on my
TV. Doing this gives me a larger view of my film to watch, and
I can watch it all the way through without the temptation of stop-
ping and making changes in the timeline. When reviewing my
films, I like to answer the following questions:

- **Did the final edited film turn out as I expected? Why or why
  not?** Here you make notes on how you feel about the final
  result of your film. Is it what you had in mind when you created the idea? Think about what is different to the original idea
  and in what ways the film did or didn't turn out as you
  expected. This is important to answer. If it didn't turn out the
  way you expected, you need to figure out why that is. Was it
  because of the scripting or storyboarding process? Or did
  changes happen during filming? Maybe your film turned out
  better than expected and nothing needs to change.

- **What would I change about the story?** This is where you can
  comment on the story. Sometimes the story ideas that work in
  our heads turn out different when acted out in a film. Did the
  story work? Did it make sense? Is there something missing? Do
  the characters work well with the story? Think about what you
  would change if you were to write the story again.

- **What would I change about the way the film looks?** Here you
  can make notes on the way the film was shot and how the footage looked in the final edit. Sometimes the footage can look
  one way during the shooting and another when imported to
  your computer. This usually comes down to the fact that
  you're looking at a small screen when filming and a larger
  screen when editing, and the larger screen magnifies everything. You may not have noticed during filming that the subject was out of focus or the lens on your camera was dirty or
  that the boom appeared in the shot. By making notes on these
  things, though, you will learn from this mistakes and take more

time checking your shots when filming your next project. You may also want to make notes about the various shots you used when filming. Do they help tell the story? Do they help to build emotions or so they distract the audience? Could you have spent more time getting the right shot or getting an extra angle? All these notes can help to make your next film look even better.

⤹ **What would I change about the process I used to make the film?** This is where you can review how the filming process went and if there is anything you would change. Were there any issues with locations or props? What was it like working with the actors and crew? Did the filming go according to plan? Did you try and fit too much into one day? Did the weather affect the filming schedule? What went well? Some things, like the weather, are not possible to control, but it's good to note down all the challenges. Remember to include what you would change when filming your next project. You may decide to have a backup plan if the weather is bad and film a different scene instead. You may aim to film less in a day or may run more rehearsals for your actors to help them develop their character and learn their lines. Don't worry if you have listed many things to change; this just helps make the filming process even better next time.

⤹ **What did I enjoy most about making this film?** This is a good opportunity to write down all the things you enjoyed about making your film from start to finish. What part of the process did you enjoy the most? Why did you enjoy making this film? What role did you enjoy within the team? What was your favorite moment? Thinking about what I enjoyed the most always reminds me of why I do this as it shows me how much I love being a filmmaker.

Remember to be positive when reviewing your film and think about all the good things about it. Being too negative about your film could cause you to lose confidence and may put you off doing another film.

Keep the review notes you make on your film and use them to develop the next project you work on.

Getting Reviews from Others

Whatever you think of your film, don't let that stop you from sharing it and getting feedback from other people. Your audience's thoughts and opinions on your film are important to the development of your skills as a filmmaker.

Aim to get as many reviews as possible. Choosing reviewers from different ages and genders will give you a clearer and more fair result. It's good if you can get some feedback from people you don't know as well, since they are more likely to openly admit how they feel about your film. People who know you often can either be too critical or negative, or too positive and can fail to highlight areas for improvement. When I started making films, I would only show a few people I knew, including my parents. This was a mistake. Because the response I got was either all positive or all negative, it was hard to reconcile the effects my film was having on the audience. I don't think these people intended to knock my confidence or put me off making films, of course, but some people tend to focus more on negative issues than the positive ones. This is why you want to get as many reviews as possible so you can choose the comments to apply to your next project. When you ask people for their opinion or to review your film, ask them for an honest opinion because they may only give you the answer you want to hear.

Another way to receive feedback and reviews is to allow people to comment on your film when you share it to YouTube or another video hosting site. Most people will give honest feedback to encourage and help you, but sometimes you may find that some people post negative or bad feedback on a video for no reason than just to try and upset you. Unfortunately, such people exist in the world. I have had some encouraging and lovely comments for the videos I've uploaded, but I've also had some really nasty comments, too. Remember to control the comments you get on your film by changing the settings when you post your video. You can choose to accept or decline the comments as they come in before they're posted below your video.

In Project 8, I showed you how to change the comments settings to approve any comments before they are posted to your video online.

To make sure you get a fair and honest review of your film, ask people to complete a review form, as shown in Figure 22-1. You can download a blank review form from this book's companion website.

Another way to get honest and useful feedback on your film is to ask professional filmmakers for their comments. There are loads of filmmakers online, many of whom may be willing to offer their thoughts on your film. An alternative to this is to submit your films into local or online film festivals. There are many different types, including youth film festivals, which would be a good place to start. At these festivals, you'll have your film viewed by people you don't know and professionals from the film and video industry. Most of these festivals will offer reviews from the judges, which is likely to be helpful and encouraging.

Try It Out Yourself

As you now review your film and think about what you have learned from making it, remember to focus on the positives from the notes you make. This may be your first film, so don't expect it to be perfect. Instead, use this experience in your next project to improve your skills as a filmmaker. Don't be nervous about showing your film to other people and asking for their comments in a review form. You can then choose if you want to use these comments in your next project.

Getting a good film review is the best feeling — it drives your creativity to write and produce more.

Film Audience Review Form

Film Title: _____

Director: _____

1) Describe your overall impressions of the film.

2) What was your opinion on the storyline? Summarize the story.

3) Describe your opinion on the production quality. *(camera angles, camerawork, sound, editing)*

4) Describe your opinion on the acting and directing.

5) What did you enjoy most about the film?

6) What genre would you class this film as? *(Action, adventure, horror, etc.)*

7) Please rate this film out of 10 *(10 being the highest)*.

Figure 22-1

Index

Notes

Notes

About the Author

Nick Willoughby is a UK-based filmmaker, director, actor, and writer who has a real enthusiasm and love for film. Nick's passion for filmmaking started when he wrote his first short film at the age of 18. Since then, he's been inspiring young people to bring their stories to life through the art of film.

Nick started his career as an actor and went on to experience a wide range of roles within the media industry, from camera operator to director. After offering his skills to schools as a film tutor and consultant, he set up Filmmaking for Kids, which aims to encourage and inspire young people to develop their creativity through the art of film. Nick now facilitates the courses at Filmmaking for Kids while writing and directing films, corporate videos, and commercials with his UK production company, 7 Stream Media.

Author's Acknowledgments

Writing *Digital Filmmaking For Kids For Dummies* was an honor and an amazing experience. So many people have supported me as a filmmaker and inspired me as a writer — too many to list on this one page.

You wouldn't have this book in your hand if it wasn't for the inspiration of executive editor Steve Hayes and the support from project manager Chris Morris. Steve and Chris have made writing this book a painless process (even if we are 4,000 miles apart).

It's been a pleasure working with a fantastic group of young filmmakers to make the films to support this book. I want to thank Ashish, Josh, Luiz, Paige, Poppy, Roo, and Skye. Their hard work, talent, whose creative ideas produced great results. Thank you to Jerome for stepping in to take a role in "Lost in Time." Thank you also to Ian for helping with some behind-the-scenes filming.

Thank you to Cassidy and my nephew Oliver for starring in some of the photos in this book.

Teamwork is essential when making films, and I have some great people around me that have supported and encouraged me. Thank you to Sean for being a great friend and business partner and for being patient with me, especially when I have my creative tantrums. Thank you to Sarah, who has been a key part in my development as a filmmaker, and who is a great friend, amazing writer, and fabulous cook.

I am especially grateful to my parents for making me who I am. Without their love, support, patience, and constructive criticism I would not be where I am today.

Lastly, I want to thank God for giving me my creative brain and for being my strength and inspiration.

Publisher's Acknowledgments

Executive Editor: Steven Hayes

Project Manager: Christopher Morris

Copy Editor: Christopher Morris

Technical Editor: Keith Underdahl

Editorial Assistant: Claire Johnson

Sr. Editorial Assistant: Cherie Case

Cover Image: ©Wiley

Apple & Mac

iPad For Dummies,
6th Edition
978-1-118-72306-7

iPhone For Dummies,
7th Edition
978-1-118-69083-3

Macs All-in-One
For Dummies, 4th Edition
978-1-118-82210-4

OS X Mavericks
For Dummies
978-1-118-69188-5

Blogging & Social Media

Facebook For Dummies,
5th Edition
978-1-118-63312-0

Social Media Engagement
For Dummies
978-1-118-53019-1

WordPress For Dummies,
6th Edition
978-1-118-79161-5

Business

Stock Investing
For Dummies, 4th Edition
978-1-118-37678-2

Investing For Dummies,
6th Edition
978-0-470-90545-6

Personal Finance
For Dummies, 7th Edition
978-1-118-11785-9

QuickBooks 2014
For Dummies
978-1-118-72005-9

Small Business Marketing
Kit For Dummies,
3rd Edition
978-1-118-31183-7

Careers

Job Interviews
For Dummies, 4th Edition
978-1-118-11290-8

Job Searching with Social
Media For Dummies,
2nd Edition
978-1-118-67856-5

Personal Branding
For Dummies
978-1-118-11792-7

Resumes For Dummies,
6th Edition
978-0-470-87361-8

Starting an Etsy Business
For Dummies, 2nd Edition
978-1-118-59024-9

Diet & Nutrition

Belly Fat Diet For Dummies
978-1-118-34585-6

Mediterranean Diet
For Dummies
978-1-118-71525-3

Nutrition For Dummies,
5th Edition
978-0-470-93231-5

Digital Photography

Digital SLR Photography
All-in-One For Dummies,
2nd Edition
978-1-118-59082-9

Digital SLR Video &
Filmmaking For Dummies
978-1-118-36598-4

Photoshop Elements 12
For Dummies
978-1-118-72714-0

Gardening

Herb Gardening
For Dummies, 2nd Edition
978-0-470-61778-6

Gardening with Free-Range
Chickens For Dummies
978-1-118-54754-0

Health

Boosting Your Immunity
For Dummies
978-1-118-40200-9

Diabetes For Dummies,
4th Edition
978-1-118-29447-5

Living Paleo For Dummies
978-1-118-29405-5

Big Data

Big Data For Dummies
978-1-118-50422-2

Data Visualization
For Dummies
978-1-118-50289-1

Hadoop For Dummies
978-1-118-60755-8

Language &
Foreign Language

500 Spanish Verbs
For Dummies
978-1-118-02382-2

English Grammar
For Dummies, 2nd Edition
978-0-470-54664-2

French All-in-One
For Dummies
978-1-118-22815-9

German Essentials
For Dummies
978-1-118-18422-6

Italian For Dummies,
2nd Edition
978-1-118-00465-4

e **Available in print and e-book formats.**

Available wherever books are sold. **For more information or to order direct visit www.dummies.com**

Math & Science

Algebra I For Dummies,
2nd Edition
978-0-470-55964-2

Anatomy and Physiology
For Dummies, 2nd Edition
978-0-470-92326-9

Astronomy For Dummies,
3rd Edition
978-1-118-37697-3

Biology For Dummies,
2nd Edition
978-0-470-59875-7

Chemistry For Dummies,
2nd Edition
978-1-118-00730-3

1001 Algebra II Practice
Problems For Dummies
978-1-118-44662-1

Microsoft Office

Excel 2013 For Dummies
978-1-118-51012-4

Office 2013 All-in-One
For Dummies
978-1-118-51636-2

PowerPoint 2013
For Dummies
978-1-118-50253-2

Word 2013 For Dummies
978-1-118-49123-2

Music

Blues Harmonica
For Dummies
978-1-118-25269-7

Guitar For Dummies,
3rd Edition
978-1-118-11554-1

iPod & iTunes
For Dummies, 10th Edition
978-1-118-50864-0

Programming

Beginning Programming
with C For Dummies
978-1-118-73763-7

Excel VBA Programming
For Dummies, 3rd Edition
978-1-118-49037-2

Java For Dummies,
6th Edition
978-1-118-40780-6

Religion & Inspiration

The Bible For Dummies
978-0-7645-5296-0

Buddhism For Dummies,
2nd Edition
978-1-118-02379-2

Catholicism For Dummies,
2nd Edition
978-1-118-07778-8

Self-Help & Relationships

Beating Sugar Addiction
For Dummies
978-1-118-54645-1

Meditation For Dummies,
3rd Edition
978-1-118-29144-3

Seniors

Laptops For Seniors
For Dummies, 3rd Edition
978-1-118-71105-7

Computers For Seniors
For Dummies, 3rd Edition
978-1-118-11553-4

iPad For Seniors
For Dummies, 6th Edition
978-1-118-72826-0

Social Security
For Dummies
978-1-118-20573-0

Smartphones & Tablets

Android Phones
For Dummies, 2nd Edition
978-1-118-72030-1

Nexus Tablets
For Dummies
978-1-118-77243-0

Samsung Galaxy S 4
For Dummies
978-1-118-64222-1

Samsung Galaxy Tabs
For Dummies
978-1-118-77294-2

Test Prep

ACT For Dummies,
5th Edition
978-1-118-01259-8

ASVAB For Dummies,
3rd Edition
978-0-470-63760-9

GRE For Dummies,
7th Edition
978-0-470-88921-3

Officer Candidate Tests
For Dummies
978-0-470-59876-4

Physician's Assistant Exam
For Dummies
978-1-118-11556-5

Series 7 Exam For Dummies
978-0-470-09932-2

Windows 8

Windows 8.1 All-in-One
For Dummies
978-1-118-82087-2

Windows 8.1 For Dummies
978-1-118-82121-3

Windows 8.1 For Dummies
Book + DVD Bundle
978-1-118-82107-7

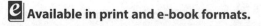 **Available in print and e-book formats.**

Available wherever books are sold. **For more information or to order direct visit www.dummies.com**

Take Dummies with you everywhere you go!

Whether you are excited about e-books, want more from the web, must have your mobile apps, or are swept up in social media, Dummies makes everything easier.

Visit Us
bit.ly/JE0O

Like Us
on.fb.me/1f1ThNu

Follow Us
bit.ly/ZDytkR

Watch Us
bit.ly/gbOQHn

Join Us
linkd.in/1gurkMm

Pin Us
bit.ly/16caOLd

Circle Us
bit.ly/1aQTuDQ

Shop Us
bit.ly/4dEp9

Leverage the Power

For Dummies is the global leader in the reference category and one of the most trusted and highly regarded brands in the world. No longer just focused on books, customers now have access to the For Dummies content they need in the format they want. Let us help you develop a solution that will fit your brand and help you connect with your customers.

Advertising & Sponsorships

Connect with an engaged audience on a powerful multimedia site, and position your message alongside expert how-to content.

Targeted ads • Video • Email marketing • Microsites • Sweepstakes sponsorship

For Dummies is a registered trademark of John Wiley & Sons, Inc.

# of For Dummies

Custom Publishing

Reach a global audience in any language by creating a solution that will differentiate you from competitors, amplify your message, and encourage customers to make a buying decision.

Apps • Books • eBooks • Video • Audio • Webinars

Brand Licensing & Content

Leverage the strength of the world's most popular reference brand to reach new audiences and channels of distribution.

For more information, visit www.Dummies.com/biz

A Wiley Brand

Dummies products make life easier!

- DIY
- Consumer Electronics
- Crafts
- Software
- Cookware
- Hobbies
- Videos
- Music
- Games
- and More!

For more information, go to **Dummies.com** and search the store by category.

For Dummies is a registered trademark of John Wiley & Sons, Inc.

FOR
DUMMIES
A Wiley Brand